ISLAND TWIST

A Carib-American Tale of Love & Culture

EMUNAH Y'SRAEL

Island Twist

Copyright © 2023 by Emunah Y'srael.

All rights reserved. Printed in the United States of America. No part of this book may be used or reproduced in any manner what soever without written permission except in the case of brief quotations em- bodied in critical articles or reviews. This book is a work of fiction. Names, characters, businesses, organiza- tions, places, events and incidents either are the product of the author's imagination or are used fictitiously. Any resemblance to actual persons, living or dead, events, or locales is entirely coincidental.

For information contact :

https://www.open-book-media.com

Book and Cover design by Emunah Y'srael
ISBN: 9798872954323

First Edition: August 2017
Second Edition : December 2023

10 9 8 7 6 5 4 3 2 1

Island Twist
Book One
Devon & Jackie

EMUNAH Y'SRAEL

for young love

Chapter One

The sun's rays beamed brightly through the open kitchen window. Spring had arrived with warm, sweet air nestled in its arms. This morning felt different. Our windows lay bare, no curtains or blinds to stop the outside world from looking in. I could hear Devon's conversation with the next-door neighbor and the chatter of children as they hurriedly made their way to school.

Whispers still rippled throughout the neighborhood about Devon and me, with absurd accusations of theft. "I promise we didn't steal the money, nor did we steal this house – the old man gave it to us." Despite the drama, I tried to ignore it all, but it still gnawed at me. In a strange way, I felt relieved that we were finally leaving this house, this city, and these people.

Imagine inheriting a house from a deceased owner. It's not that we're ungrateful, but it was a tough situation. We had little money, no furniture, just the house. We moved in during the winter, and the hardwood floors felt like ice. The pipes froze frequently, and we couldn't afford the high oil prices. Devon suggested we layer our clothing instead of turning up the heat. It may sound cheap, but he terms it as being frugal. It's amazing the lengths we'll go to for love. There were times when I wanted to ask my parents for a space heater, but I didn't want to embarrass my husband.

As I stood in the kitchen, I couldn't help but notice the clean but outdated decor. The counter was adorned with accent tiles featuring farm animals and barns, but it was clear that the space needed a fresh coat of paint and a new floor. Despite its imperfections, we knew that this kitchen would serve the next family just as well as it had served us.

Devon returned looking agitated, and although I was supposed to be packing so we could hit the road, I felt exhausted.

"Sweetie, don't forget to get the last box please, it's over in the corner." He pointed to a box labeled "fragile," filled with carefully wrapped crystal hangings and folded lilac curtains precious mementos from our wedding day.

"Yes, babes," I motioned toward the living room to gather the things. Suddenly, my knees gave out and my head swam with dizziness.

"What's going on?" asked my husband, who was standing nearby.

"I don't know," I replied, struggling to regain my composure. Despite my efforts, the overwhelming emotion continued to affect me.

"Take a seat Jackie, I'll get it."

He is so caring; did I mention how much I love my husband? Even after ten years of marriage, the sound of his voice still strums the strings that make my heart sing. I can't believe that I ever wanted to be with his cousin! But that's a long story for another time.

Taking a seat at the wooden table wedged in the corner of our kitchen, I couldn't help but reminisce. This table – our beloved kitchen table – had served us well. It was rescued by Devon from a curb on his way home one night. Although I wasn't convinced about bringing roadside furniture into our home, Devon patiently sanitized, sanded and painted it each night after work, insisting that it would look good if only I gave it a chance. And he was right.

The table proved to be useful, too. Devon studied here many a day, and I found it to be the perfect size for my art and sewing projects. Our babies ate their first meal here, often making a real mess. If you look closely enough, you can still see Samuel's note, "I love mom," written with a permanent marker. His twin sister Leah followed suit and carved her love note, filling it with glitter and glue for added flair. I was upset that day, but their father said, "leave it alone because they were just expressing themselves." He even claimed that it gives the table character.

Our love was like this table, and I would have never guessed that something so right could start off so wrong. Despite everything that happened, we were overjoyed to have a place to live, and start our family. It wasn't easy, and sometimes I still wonder how we stayed together despite the rumors and all the people who wanted to see us fail.

CHAPTER TWO

The fact is my husband inherited this house from the elder who owned it and counted him as a son. When Devon's family first migrated from the Caribbean, they moved to a home a few blocks away from a man named Mr. Carleton. He lived in this beautifully maintained single-family home. The lawn was always well manicured, and everyone admired it. The thing that really stuck out about Mr. Carleton was he lived alone; he never married and never had any children.

Strange, huh?

Mr. Carleton was an unusual man, silent, tall, and mysterious. He retired the same year that Devon moved to America. He always said he was forced to retire from his job as a senior maintenance manager because, "he was too old to have around anymore." That job meant a lot to him, Devon says he never got over it, which probably explains why most days you could find him sweeping and cleaning even when the place was already clean.

Other than Mr. Carleton's love affair with cleanliness, the only thing he loved to do more was people watch. Around noon every day, after his mid-morning nap, you could find him in his favorite chair peering through his kitchen window watching the world pass by. As he aged, he lost his mobility, Devon always volunteered to help him out before and after school. He would run his errands and do his shopping. My husband's parents wondered what he was doing at the ol' man's house all the time, but never stopped him from going.

"Be careful, yuh neva can trust people; him too quiet," his mother warned.

The neighborhood women would whisper and talk about Mr. Carleton all the time.

Something wrong with him why him neva married?

They couldn't figure him out.

Even in his golden years, it was obvious that Mr. Carleton was a handsome man. He still had all his teeth and a head full of jet-black curly hair. He made for an intriguing character and neighborhood women busied themselves weaving all manner of tales about him.

One story goes that some years ago, when Mr. Carleton was much younger, the women decided to send in a decoy to test him out. Miss Mavis Fields volunteered because secretly she thought he was handsome and wanted an excuse to get closer to him. So, one day she got dressed up and 'sweet up herself' with perfume. Each of the ladies watched her not so discreetly from their front porch as Miss Mavis made her way over to Mr. Carleton's front door and rang the bell. When he finally answered, she introduced herself.

"Hey, Mr. Carleton, I am Sister Mavis. I heard a lot about you."

"Yeh," he replied not even looking her way.

"I am new to the neighborhood and wanted to meet all my neighbors." She continued, not quite ready to give up her mission.

"Nice to meet you and thanks for coming," his response was lackluster at best.

"Aren't you going to invite me in for a drink or something?"

"In where?" he retorted.

"Madam I don't know you; you could be a mad woman for all I know."

"But I..." before she could convince him otherwise, *BAM!* He slammed the door loudly in her face.

The ladies who were watching in suspense suddenly erupted into fits of laughter at Miss Mavis' epic fail with Mr. Carleton.

Devon seemed to be the only person who he allowed to get close to him. He became like the grandson he never had, and Mr. Carleton was genuinely grateful to Devon for all his help. He lived at 198 Newhall Ave, which was in one of the better and more beautiful areas in Queens.

Mr. Carleton died two weeks after Devon graduated from university. He was a meticulous man and he had already finalized all his burial arrangements so there was no need for any fuss. Even though his neighbors never had an opportunity to get close to him, many long-time associates came to the funeral, some out of concern and some out of curiosity, eager to find out what would become of the "dead left."

The funeral was quiet and uneventful. The service had a full house, but no family members showed up.

The following week, Devon received a certified letter in the mail, summoning him to the office of Attorney Basil Thompson. He racked his brain for any high school indiscretion he might have gotten into, but he had never been in any real trouble. Maybe the letter was meant for his cousin Trevor, who never changed his official address even though he rarely came around anymore.

I remember that phone call; the sky had darkened, and it was set to rain all day. Around 3 pm that afternoon thunder and lightning began to roll in.

"Jackie a letter came here for me, from a lawyer," his voice overflowing with concern.

"A lawyer!"

"Jackie come off de phone," my mother bellowed.

"You nuh see thunder and lightning!"

"I can't stay long, so talk quick. What did you do?"

He sounded upset so I suggested that I accompany him to the lawyer's office. Devon agreed and came by my parents' house the next day to pick me up; together we arrived at Esquire Basil Thompson's office at noon sharp.

It is funny how much my parents have changed since I graduated from college. Only in my wildest dreams could 'man' come and pick me up before now. Any who, as soon as we arrived at Mr. Thompson's office, we were greeted by his receptionist.

"Is Mr. Thompson in?"

"Is who you?" she asked, while eyeing us up and down.

"Is who me? Um, I am here to see Mr. Thompson; is he in?" Devon answered, equally unimpressed with her lack of professionalism.

"No need to get snappy sar," she replied.

"Him inna de back," pointing her finger towards the slightly ajar office door off to the side. Her candy red nails sailed through the air; they curved like claws at the ends. My red-carpet rundown of Rita the receptionist was cut short by the sound of Devon's voice.

"Can you get him, or at least call him for us?" Devon asked, still expecting some kind of formality from her.

"Just go ahead," she responded, waving us off.

As we approached the door, we heard what sounded like Mr. Thompson laughing and whispering into his phone.

"No worries my wife will never know. I will call you later."

Then there was a lip-smacking sound followed by more whispering.

Devon and I looked at one another; we shrugged our shoulders and decided we should knock on three.

1, 2, 3

Knock, knock

The door whined as it slowly opened wider.

Clank!

The receiver crashed loudly when Mr. Thompson abruptly slammed it down. We must have startled him because we could hear the rustling of papers as he clumsily shuffled through the documents strewn all over his desk. He grabbed one at random and began staring at it with exaggerated concentration.

"Eh em ...Who is it?" He called from behind his desk.

"I'm Devon Clarke and this is my fiancé, Jackie, we have a 12 o'clock appointment."

I felt annoyed as Devon gave our introduction and announced his schedule to the lawyer, wasn't this something that the secretary should be doing.

"Yes, yes come in," his tone was professional, if forced.

We stepped through the door together, but I stopped short, halted mid stride by a rancid smell.

What is that smell?

I had to stop myself from curling my lip in disgust.

What have we stepped into?

Devon nudged me and I stepped inside hesitantly. Surveying the cramped office, I began to take inventory; one dated green shag carpet lined the floor, layers of dust blanketed the furnishings, striped lime green velvet curtains blocking any hope of fresh air from coming in the windows. The florescent light bulbs flickered while making the most annoying buzzing sound. At any moment now Mr. Lawyer-man would be left in the dark.

Whenever someone stood out to me it was inevitable that I would rename them. Sometimes, the nicknames would accurately reflect some aspect about the person and sometimes it would be a facetious play on it. There was nothing about this man or this place that said "lawyer." The garbage can beside his desk was overflowing with crumpled paper and what appeared to be scraps of three-day old chow mien. I felt myself gasping for air as I desperately scanned the room for some hidden window, so that the possibility of fresh air and light could seep in, but there was no such thing.

The tightening grip of Devon's hand in mine jarred me away from my health inspection. I refocused my attention back to our host and the reason for our visit today.

"Have a seat and relax." he motioned.

Relax? You have got to be kidding!

Ok, you got me. I can be a bit scornful in 'dirty' places. I did not want to sit, and Devon knew it. Blame my upbringing, but me and dirt were not friends and the way those chairs looked there was a very real possibility I could catch something just from sitting down. Devon nudged me to sit. I obliged, perching at the very edge of the chair.

My heart skipped several beats as I wondered what this was all about; the sweat from my palms made it easy for me to slip my hands away from my fiance's. The handle of the chair that I grabbed to keep my balance was also covered with moisture. I looked over at Devon to find him twitching his left foot and cracking his knuckles.

Why would a lawyer want to see Devon?

Finally, Mr. Thompson broke the silence.

"Do you know why you are here?"

I shook my head and Devon answered, "No."

"Well, it is about Mr. Carleton."

At the mention of Mr. Carleton, Devon let out a laborious and sorrowful sigh.

What was this lawyer driving at? I was growing impatient but had no choice but to wait.

"Mr. Carleton? He died a few weeks ago," Devon lamented.

He was still mourning the loss of his elder and friend and expressed that he learned so much from him; Mr. Carleton was like his grandfather.

Patience is a virtue, Jackie, I reminded myself silently.

The lawyer nodded then stood up and walked a few paces over to a safe in the corner that was practically buried between a stack of loose papers and folders. We watched as he lazily shuffled all the folders from one side to the other.

Did this man know we were coming? Didn't he call us? I mumbled to no one in particular.

I wasn't sure how much longer I could hold my breath without passing out. The lawyer stopped suddenly, and our attention was drawn to his direction. He started speaking aloud.

"I am sorry Mr. Thompson, are you talking to us?" Devon asked.

"No, no, I am just trying to remember the code," he muttered as he leaned against the wall and stared at the safe.

I became increasingly annoyed and unwittingly used my tongue to kiss the back of my front teeth. The man was as aggravating and unprofessional as his receptionist. Through my peripheral vision, I could see Devon drifting off. I tried to discreetly get his attention, but he never looked my way.

Meanwhile, back at the safe, Mr. Lawyer-man was still finagling with the combination. *Come one man didn't you know we were coming!*

Unprofessionalism, of any sort, has always been a major pet-peeve of mine and this lawyer's office was my, all-time-number-one worst experience to date. This guy was even worse than the woman at the patty shop by the college who got a nasty attitude because I said she sold me a 'bun up' two-day old patty. Can you believe she tried to get me banned from her establishment?

Finally, I heard the sweetest sound coming from the corner *click, click, click, pop*! After much anticipation, the safe was opened. Mr. Thompson retrieved a black envelope with a gold clasp from under a load of other important-looking documents. *Must he do everything so slowly?* I began to think he was doing it to spite us; his actions seemed deliberate.

The lawyer strolled over to his desk, and flung the envelope on the table before asking us in a condescending tone, "Do you know what this is?"

I wanted to say, *why do you keep asking questions we obviously don't know the answer to*? But, instead, I let Devon speak since I was just a guest accompanying him. The stuffy office space began to close in on me. I was hot and the dust was irritating my sinuses. Mr. Thompson must have noticed me fidgeting because after some time of squirming in my seat he finally popped the question,

"Would you both like something to drink?"

Even though the service so far has been horrible, I couldn't hold out anymore. My throat was parched and under much environmental duress, I agreed to a drink. Only moments after accepting the offer did I realize it may have been safer to wait.

"Rita," he shouted, "Come get our clients some wata from round a back!"

Clients? Who were his clients and what did he mean by 'round a back'?

No, I screamed silently, not Rita the receptionist from the front desk. I hoped the water was bottled; *please let the water be bottled*. That was a vain hope that lasted all of two seconds. To my dismay, the water came brimming to the top in a questionable glass from some unknown water source "round a back." It was nerve wrecking to watch her navigate her way from the door to where we were seated. At any moment, I expected the water would spill over on us. She found her way towards Devon's side and stretched seductively over him. If I wasn't mistaken her breast brushed his face.

To make matters worse, when I asked her for a straw she replied, "Yeh lady, no problem," then proceeded to reach under her left arm to retrieve two straws with their wrappers already removed. Rita then performed yet another 'stretch and brush move' over my fiancé to hand them to me.

I mustered up every ounce of home training to ignore these provocations and muttered through clenched teeth, "Thank you."

"My pleasure ma'am," She replied sheepishly,

This day was getting worse and all I wanted by then was to get this meeting over with. I pretended to take a sip for appearances' sake and offered some to Devon, but he waved me off; he didn't want any either it seemed. We both turned our attention to Mr. Thompson, letting him know it was alright to proceed.

"Well," he began, while facing Devon, "Who is Mr. Carleton to you?"

"He is, I mean was, my neighbor" Devon answered.

"How long have you known him?" Mr. Thompson pressed.

"Since my family moved here some twelve years ago." Devon replied.

"Wait is this some kind of police investigation," I blurted, springing from my chair.

Devon shot me a stern look and hinted for me to calm down. I sat back in my chair and began to rub my sweaty palms together. *Will this man just get to the point.*

Mr. Thompson chuckled and continued his line of questioning. He wanted to know who I was and how long we had been engaged, etc.

After much inquiry, even Devon began to grow weary, "Sir why are we here?"

"Confirmation, my friend, just need a bit of confirmation. I have to mek sure we have the right person."

"The right person, for what?" Devon replied.

"Well," he responded.

"Your neighbor, Mr. Carleton, as you know had no children and you were like a grandson to him. He wrote a will and wanted me to read it to you after his passing."

Devon had learned all about what had happened to Mr. Carleton's family; he lost contact with them once he came to America. When he arrived in New York, he decided not to marry again, and worked and lived his life in solitude. When Devon came along the elder regretted not having someone to give his wealth to and so in his will, he named my fiancé Devon as the beneficiary to his entire estate.

Mr. Lawyer-man cleared his throat and with enough bass to make the walls tremble began to read:

"Devon Clarke, I Elroy Carleton bequeath to you my home at 198 Newhall Ave, Rosedale, New York. This home is for you to take possession of and upkeep to the standard detailed below effective upon your marriage to your fiancée Jackie Brown."

Unbeknownst to me, Mr. Carleton and Devon had many conversations about our relationship over the years. He often warned Devon not to end up like him by thinking that money and success was more important than building a family and encouraged him to invest in solid relationships. Although I knew virtually nothing about Mr. Carleton, apparently, he knew a lot about me and was a guiding influence for many choices that Devon made over the years.

Devon and I looked at each other slack jawed, but Mr. Thompson was oblivious to our amazement and determined to continue reading. He effectively interrupted our sidebar moment.

"Shall I go on?" he asked, barely hiding his disapproval at our apparent lack of attention. "Eh, emm," the lawyer huffed, then assumed an official air that really didn't suit him as he continued reading,

"Also, there are monies that will be dispersed at one-year intervals with which you are to use to maintain the unit and pay taxes. In the interim, you are to start your career and work your way up so that you will understand the value of earning a dollar for yourself. I have included an engagement gift to help toward the expenses of planning your wedding. I would have loved to be there in person, but since I can't please accept this gift in advance."

The first disbursement concerning the house will be given after you move in. The home will have no furniture; you must start from scratch filling it with love. After remaining "happily married," for ten years you will receive a lump sum of $100,000, at which time you can move on, rent out but never sell the property."

I nearly fell over on the desk and came very close to knocking the nasty water all over the floor. Devon's face looked exactly like it did in the sixth grade when Ms. Margaret called on him to explain what he thought about 'birds and the bees' video she had just shown the class. I tried to whisper his name, but he was non-responsive.

We were both at a loss for words. The last thing I remember hearing is Mr. Lawyer-man saying he would be the acting attorney over the will to ensure that the wishes of Mr. Carleton were carried out. The lawyer reached across his cluttered desk and handed Devon his card.

"You and I will become well acquainted over the next few years. Here are my contact numbers, feel free to call me any time."

Devon reached for the card and as he leaned forward to retrieve his wallet from his back pocket, the lawyer looked straight into my eyes and winked at me. That wink made my whole-body shudder, and he got mentally filed away with his trashy office and receptionist. I couldn't wait to get out of there.

We both rose from our chairs and thanked him for his time.

"I will be in touch," Devon said.

"Good day sar and ma'am," called Rita as she closed the door behind them.

Chapter Three

I admit that I am not the friendliest person, but that's not the reason that Rita and Mr. Lawyer-man rubbed me the wrong way. I'm sure that Devon dismissed my behavior that day to the picky personality he has grown accustomed to, but a woman's intuition is one thing that men mistakenly take too lightly.

To his credit though, Devon does know me better than most people and understands why I don't open easily to new people. To be honest, I don't really understand the appeal of having a wide circle of friends. I learned early on that having a lot of friends was not going to be a big part of my life.

"Friends! You don't need friends; look, see, you have brothers and sisters, they are good enough." This was my parents' mantra. I often wondered why they had such an aversion to the F word. It was almost as if some childhood experience of untrustworthy friends played over and over, like a broken record in their heads. Every time the word was mentioned they frowned. I wondered about who could give me better insight into why they were that way, I considered my grandparents, but I reasoned that they would probably just repeat what seemed to be our family motto.

The first time I realized this was going to be a problem I was around nine and a little girl named Selah befriended me. We sat beside one another in class, ate lunch together, and giggled while watching the boys during recess. Selah was a thoughtful girl and very kind. Her mother was our local celebrity chef, she was known as Chef Sebastian, and she would often make surprise trips to our class giving each of us one of her famous chocolate chip cookies.

One day, Mrs. Sebastian brought us a special treat and gave everyone extra cookies to take home to their family. Selah gave my bag to me with a card attached. I was curious about the pretty card; it was multi-colored with confetti streamers and the words "Brown Family" neatly written by hand on the front.

"Give this to your parents when you get home." she said.

"I will," I replied.

I was so excited that day that I ran inside to meet my parents screaming, "Mama, dada, look!"

"What's this?" Mama snatched the bag and card that I was holding.

I found that question strange since simply opening the package would reveal what it was.

"Open it nuh dear," urged Dada.

Mama struggled to open the envelope neatly along the flap without tearing it. When she finally did, she removed a delicate looking card and began shrieking.

"INVITE! What kinda thing this?"

It was a cordial invitation to an opening celebration for the new café Selah's family bought downtown. I could smell the cookies and my mouth salivated as I imagined waiting to be offered one. Then mama opened the bag.

"Cookies!" she barked in disgust.

"Humph, you don't need any cookies. I will hold on to these."

A tight knot formed in my throat. I opened my mouth to speak but nothing came out. I tried again this time something came out scratchy but audible, "Mama, what about the invite? Can we go?"

"Go, go where?" she snapped.

I always wondered why she repeated what you said only to say it again louder. Maybe it was for dramatic effect; mama was dramatic a lot. It looked as if she was taking a minute to deliberate; then she turned to look at my father, both had disturbed expressions on their faces. I watched them, looking first at my mother and then at my father and stood there eager to hear the verdict. It would be great if we could go. My siblings would enjoy it and I would get to visit my friend Selah. Who could say no to free cookies?

Finally, after what felt like hours of silence mama delivered an unequivocal, "No!"

No? Did she say what I think she said? Immediately tears began to flow from my eyes, snot ran down my nose, and I lost all control.

"Why not mama?" I cried. "She is my friend!"

There it was. I said it-the dreaded F word and boy did it set her off that day. There is no doubt that my family contributed to my own anti-social behavior.

Nothing really changed until I turned sixteen. Tanya and I met at soccer tryouts during the spring of that year. You see even though I wasn't allowed to have a social life, my parents didn't mind me playing sports. As you can imagine, I tried out every sport available, badminton, tennis, soccer, and even cross-country track. Athletics was my only escape. For the first time in my life, I was finally allowed to have a friend; we were real friends, meaning she could call my house and occasionally, I was allowed to visit hers.

My house was, wow, how should I describe it? Well, let me just say interesting. I am the fifth child. My name was the one they often forgot. Imagine being called the names of four children before they got to the person they really wanted. You would think that was the crazy part about being the last child, until one day it turns out that maybe I wouldn't be the last child after all, after almost two decades I was informed I was getting a little brother.

"Mama are you pregnant at 58?" I blurted out one day.

She laughed heartily and responded, "No, Jackie."

I was confused. They said we were getting a new brother, but mama wasn't pregnant. Dada sat me down and explained that they were adopting a young boy who needed a loving home. Now that all their own children were nearly grown, they decided to adopt a young boy in need, give him some structure, and a safe place to live.

Our house ran like a military base. Household chores were delegated so that every member of the house shared in the responsibility of its upkeep. There was never any excuse for the home to be untidy. The boys oversaw sweeping the yard and taking out the trash every night and the girls each took a week on bathroom duty. When my sisters left home, I picked up their dish washing days, Tuesday, Thursday, and Sunday. The bathroom chores fell on me alone. *Do you have any idea what it feels like to clean up after a house full of people?* It seems that no matter how old your brothers get, they still can't seem to aim straight. Nothing makes you want to move out like cleaning toilets decorated with pee drops every week. *I mean, how hard is it to lift and flush?*

I loved my family and, yes, there is something great about having a big ol mess of them, but I must confess, I often dreamt of a quiet home, in the countryside where I could sleep late and live a simple yet quiet life.

Chapter Four

Mornings—let's see, oh yes, grogginess, agitation all things not good or chipper like. My eyes blinked repeatedly to remove the tiny yellow crust that formed in the corners of my eyes overnight. Drool saturated my pillow as always when the sleep was so sweet that I couldn't seem to control my mouth water. It didn't help that my bunk bed was positioned against the radiator which ran from the floor to the ceiling in the 'girls' room' that I once shared with my sisters. Whenever it was wintertime, I would awaken drenched in sweat. No matter how many times we complained, the landlord only provided two temperatures, freezing cold or hell hot. Dada chose the latter and we adjusted to it.

These days I had *the girls' room* all to myself ever since my second oldest sister Lena recently went on to college and the oldest Tamar got married; the jury is still out on whether she is 'happily married' or not.

It was a school day, but by now I had hit the snooze button about three times already. I could hear my brother's footsteps nearing my room; he had the most irritating habit of busting in first, then banging on the already breached door.

"Get up! Get up Jackie or else," he threatened.

"Or else, what?" I challenged.

I can't stand it when he does that; everyone knows that I am not exactly a peppy morning person. Why must he be so loud? I was going to answer him in a not so nice manner and just as I gathered enough waking strength to tell him a thing or two, I heard my father calling me.

"Jackie, my princess you up?"

"Yes Dada," I answered without a hint of grogginess.

"Tidy, up yourself and come here. I have something I need you to do for me later." He called from the kitchen.

Hearing dada's voice, I sprang into action. I hurriedly tidied up and got ready for school. I found my father seated at the kitchen table drinking hot cinnamon tea as usual and reading the morning paper. Mama was preparing breakfast.

"Morning dada, morning mama," I chirped.

"Morning Jackie," they responded in unison.

"Hurry and have some tea and breakfast," said mama. "You are late, and your brothers are getting ready to leave you."

I was already halfway through my senior year of high school and my twin older brothers were in their second year of college. Since it wasn't out of the way, they gave me a ride to school in the morning, but if I was late, they would threaten to leave me. On days that they made good on it, I would have to walk the seven blocks to school by myself. Unlike a lot of classmates, I really enjoyed school. I just couldn't figure out why it had to start so early. School gave me a chance to get out of the house and see children my own age.

I packed a bite to eat, bid my parents goodbye and grabbed an extra sweater on my way out the door. I rushed up the block to meet my brothers who were sitting in the car as it warmed up. The music streamed from the cracked window. I rolled my eyes while reaching to open the door. As much as I love reggae, it was too early for the bassline to stir and vibrate every cell in my body.

"Turn it down please," I yelled beating the back of Jazz's passenger seat.

He didn't even bother to turn back; he just waved me off and started to bop his head more. It was futile; I sunk into the back seat and endured the noise until I got to school. When we pulled up, they both made sure to warn me to stay away from *"dem duty bwoys dem a school"* or they would tell mama and dada about me. I waved them off, but not before they hurled one last insult to remind me, I was still their little sister.

Jazz rolled down his window and yelled mockingly, "Have a good day *mawga Jackie*." I could hear him and Marcus laughing all the way up until I reached the front door of the school.

As mama would say, I was a "very slender girl." Not skinny, or "mawga" but petite. The other girls at school had long developed their womanly physique and I, well, I was a late bloomer. I'd been waiting for "Aunt Flow" ever since I was in the sixth grade. That year, school sent us home with permissions slips that allowed them to show a "birds and bees" presentation in class. My parents signed it reluctantly and mumbled something about "what kinda slackness are they teaching in school."

I wondered why they called puberty "slackness," but I never worked up enough courage to find out. For the next six years, my mother was silent on the matter of menstruation, and I watched intently for the day it would arrive.

Chapter Five

Devon had a crush on me since the sixth grade, but, back then, I couldn't get beyond his round belly, tight pants, and nerdy looking glasses. He was overly sensitive to the prospect of me liking, or being liked by, anyone except him and he would often sabotage any potential "in school" love interest.

Trevor was Devon's cousin, who moved from the Caribbean to live with his family earlier this year. Trevor had smooth ebony skin kissed by the Island sun. His deep voice and Jamaican accent had all the girls fawning. It was crush at first sight, all the girls wanted him, including me. At lunchtime, I would wait in the cafeteria to see where he and Devon were sitting. Then Tanya and I would sit close enough to hear their conversations but far enough not to appear *thirsty* and obvious.

Trevor and I had biology class together, but I don't even think that he noticed. However, my interest in him did not go unnoticed by Devon, who grew jealous and competitive over my attention. I remember one morning; my father asked me to stop at the cleaners to pick up his suit. Now Devon's house was on the way from school to the cleaners, I must have passed his place hundreds of times over the years, but something felt different now that Trevor lived there. I found myself anticipating a chance meeting where I would accidentally be bumping into him.

While running my father's errand that day, I happened to see Trevor and Devon sitting outside on their front stoop. My eyes fell instantly on Trevor and suddenly everything seemed to be moving in slow motion. We weren't in school, and this was the first time I had encountered Trevor in *real life*. I approached them with an even pace, trying to be *cute*.

Should I wave and keep walking? Or casually stop and say hello? I wasn't sure how or if I should make myself known to him, until I heard him say, "There she is," Devon shouted while pointing in my direction.

"She is the one that has a big ol' crush on you Trevor!"

Wait, Huh? And just like that I was exposed. Devon... *ahhh.* I couldn't believe him, my stomach teemed with butterflies. Frozen in humiliation, disoriented, and fuming, I made a mental note to give Devon a piece of my mind later. After what felt like an eternity, I mustered up enough courage to lift my head up only to find Devon staring menacingly back at me.

Fe me and fe him eye mek four, as old-time people would say. My gaze remained locked with his, but my stomach began to churn with increasing intensity, as if it were trying to tell me something. Suddenly, a warm, undeniable urge washed over me. I knew what it meant, and I took off running for home. My mother was taken aback when I barged in, greeting her with nothing more than a curt hello before dashing to the bathroom. When I finally arrived, I was both relieved and shocked. It had arrived late but finally here. That moment marked my official induction into womanhood, a feeling of excitement mixed with fear. I had forgotten the video's advice long ago, and so I frantically called for my mother.

"Mama," I need you. My mother came to the door in a hurry.

"What happen?"

"It's here." I showed where I had sullied myself. The silence was deafening, mama stood there and just stared as if I had injured myself. She left the bathroom without a word and returned shortly with a small package of sanitary napkins.

"Use these," she said and don't tell anyone your business."

I was bewildered, what was that about? I had older sisters, but they never told me much either, they took care of their time of the month discreetly and without much complaint. I wondered why the secrecy. *A secret from whom and why?* I tried not to think too much about the reasons because, to me, this was great, it meant I would finally grow some boobs and get a little shape to my body. *Welcome to womanhood Jackie Brown.*

Chapter Six

The next few months were difficult as I did my best to avoid Devon and Trevor as much as possible. Don't get it twisted, I still had a huge crush on Trevor, but I struggled with how to get pass Devon's watchful eye. I even changed my route going home, taking the long way just to avoid seeing the cousins together. My parents started to suspect something was wrong because I was always late getting home. Graduation came and went without repeating the *red run* incident.

-~-

"Jackie, please come here princess," Dada called. He wanted me to go on another errand to the cleaners.

I was so apprehensive about running into Devon or Trevor that I even protested a little, which I rarely ever did, especially when it came to my father.

"I need you to pick up and take something to the cleaners Jackie, and I don't want you coming in late either." said Dada.

"I..." I fumbled searching for an excuse but failed, "ok Dada," I reluctantly agreed.

The idea of having to pass by Devon's house freaked me out, but my father had made it clear that I should go and come back quickly. On my way to get dressed I heard mama calling me from her room.

"Yes mama?"

I pushed the door to her room and found her sitting in her favorite spot, bent over her beloved antique sewing machine and listening to WNEWS FM on the radio. She motioned with her hand for me to come closer. Mama rose from her chair and made her way over to her fabric station which was brimming with vibrant colors and beautiful prints; she stepped up on her stool, with difficulty, even stumbling a bit while reaching for the material she needed.

"Mama, are you alright?" I called out to her watching to make sure she had regained her balance.

She never answered or looked at me; I watched as she stood on her tippy toes determined to reach for the fabric way at the top of the pile. Once she had the fabric in hand, she hastily attempted to get down, missing a step and nearly stumbled onto the floor. She reached out to steady herself; I reached out just in time to prevent her from getting seriously hurt.

During the commotion mama grabbed my shoulder tightly with her free hand and dug her fingers in with enough force to make me think she might have dislocated it. During her flailing, she kicked my shin sending my own foot sliding back until my baby toe smacked hard against the iron leg of the sewing machine. Talk about pain! I wanted to yell and cry all at once, but, instead, I settled for a whimper.

Aww, I that hurt!

"Hush, baby I am sorry, I don't know what happened."

She felt ashamed of her tumble and wanted to get back to her work as soon as possible. My mother, who was not very tall, but had a feisty and formidable personality, was embarrassed about the fall. "Come here baby," she said as if nothing had happened, "look at the fabric your father bought for you. Isn't it beautiful?"

I limped over to get a better look at the fabric, not quite able to forget about the stool incident with my still throbbing toe. I managed to mumble, "Yes, mama, it's pretty."

"Good, I am going to make you a new dress," Mama said decidedly. I nodded my head in acknowledgement and forced a smile for my mother's sake.

"Are you ready to go to the cleaners for your father now?" Mama asked.

Huh? They still wanted me to go after getting my toe smashed with nothing but a "hush" to soothe the pain! I dared not to express my discontent with what I thought was a very unreasonable request. Instead, I limped out of her room, into mine, and got ready to leave.

Summer was here, and Valley High was officially over. I was eager to start City College in the fall and missed school a bit. Most of all, I missed Trevor – my crush. It had been weeks since graduation, and I was curious whether I'd run into him again. Everything had been quiet lately. Devon went missing after senior year, which was great. However, I hadn't seen Trevor either. Just the thought of him still made me tingle.

While in my room, I tried rubbing the pain out of my toe. I grabbed my favorite dress, the "sunflower delight," from my closet and put it on for my errand. On my way out of the room, my reflection caught my eye. I doubled back to take a good look in the full-length mirror near my door, *yep I'm fly*.

"Jackie," Dada called again.

"Come take this money and my suit to the cleaners."

"Ok, Dada,"

As I made my way towards him, the phone rang.

"Ansa di phone," Mama ordered from her room.

"Good afternoon, Brown residence," I answered.

"Hey, who is this? Tamar? Lena? Jazz? Marcus?" I could not help but roll my eyes as the caller ran down a list of my siblings.

"No," I responded, "this is Jackie; may I ask who is calling?"

"You don't recognize my voice?" the caller replied.

Giving the caller a bit of feistiness or as some would call it "sass" was tempting, but I decided against it, concluding that she was likely an adult that knew my parents.

"May I ask whom you would like to speak with," I asked politely.

"Jackie, oh it's you! My how you sound like big girl so, well this is your Auntie Dolores from country."

Who is Auntie Dolores from the country? I was puzzled without a single clue who I was speaking to. My family left the island some years ago when I was still young. I knew that it was customary to sometimes call friends of the family *uncle or auntie* as a sign of respect. Could she be one of those? Then again, she could be one of any number of women my uncle Ricky kept around him, they were also introduced to us as "auntie" instead of terms more accurate but less appropriate for young ears. At any rate, I didn't have time to figure it out and I gave "Auntie Dolores from country" the option of speaking to either my mother or father. She chose to speak with my mother. I handed mama the phone and made my way to the cleaners.

The sunshine burst through the front door. The Mister Softee ice-cream truck chimed in the distance. There were little girls and boys dressed in beachwear making their way toward the fire hydrant across the street. An older boy was walking towards the hydrant with a big wrench, ready to crack it open. I knew I had to move quickly if I didn't want to get wet. I hurriedly made my way down the steps and up the street, still limping a bit because of my bruised toe.

No sooner than my foot hit the pavement, I heard the annoying sound of someone yelling my name loudly from behind.

"Jackie Brown!"

My heart began to pound as I contemplated running with each beat. There was only one person I knew that said my name like that. I slowly turned in the direction of the voice and sure enough it was Devon. I made a quick and discreet scan to see if he was alone. I wasn't sure if I could face Trevor like this after the last time we met or kind of met, well you know after the "red run" encounter.

"Where you been pretty young thang?" tumbled awkwardly off Devon's lips.

I wondered if he had hit his head. Devon had gotten some new "gear." He wore his hat turned to the side, and his shirt unbuttoned several spaces from the collar; I could even see the beginning of some chest hair peeking through behind his gold chain.

"I am alright," I responded nervously not sure where to look.

Devon tried to use more of the American slang he picked up, which made me very uncomfortable; I was used to his normal high-pitched Jamaican patios.

"Why do you keep looking over your shoulder, you a run from police?" he teased sounding more like himself.

"No, um I have to run an errand for my father."

I began walking briskly down the street. Devon followed.

We stopped up the block from the cleaners. I decided to give him a chance to speak his peace. He was quiet while he tried to catch his breath, I had no idea what to say to him, until finally I worked up enough nerve to ask, "So, where is your cousin?"

Devon's easy-going demeanor melted away, his nostrils flared and a bead of sweat suddenly gathered on his forehead.

"Why are you always asking about him?" he asked visibly irritated.

I began to take slow steps backwards; the change in his voice frightened me a bit. Devon put his hands on his round waist and took a deep breath. I watched him intently; he reached into his pocket and took out a large ball of five cent peppermint.

The silence between us was broken by the rustling of the candy wrapper. Before I knew it, I had inadvertently backed into the gate, the drycleaning clutched in my hand waiting to see what Devon would say next.

The gate behind me was much taller than I was; He towered over me and leaned in closer, placing his palms on the bars of the gate above my head. Now I was even more uncomfortable, what if someone passed by and saw me '*talk to man*' like this? A barrage of '*what ifs*' flooded my mind, just as the menthol from Devon's breath brought me back to my senses.

"Jackie, you know how long I've liked you and I want you to be my wife."

Seh wah, be your who? Have you lost your mind? I didn't say what I was thinking, but I didn't make any effort to hide it on my face either.

"Your wife?" I repeated. *I am not allowed to have boyfriends much less a husband and who says it would be you anyway?*

Boy I never thought I would see the day that I would be grateful for one of my parents' many rules.

"Come on, Jackie I see the way you look at my cousin. Don't mind him. I am the one for you." Devon said, once again reminding me how closely he was monitoring my crush on Trevor and how much it animated his competitive side.

"Mek me and you get married one day," he suggested.

Surprised and flustered, I quickly changed the subject.

"What time is it, Devon?"

"3:15," he answered after consulting the watch on his wrist.

"3:15." I echoed, scooting across the gate until I was no longer tented under him, and I shouted over my shoulder, "I have to go, I can't be late." I took off running, or more like hobbling quickly up the block, relieved to be free of Devon's penetrating stare.

Dinner was already cooking, and my parents were sitting together watching the five o'clock news. I never really got the point of the news; it's always depressing, so I usually avoid it. Instead, I spend my time in my room doing my artwork or writing poetry. Since school was out, there were no sports events to attend, which meant I was stuck at home with no social life. I was getting anxious to talk to someone, anyone, about my crush on Trevor, and how his cousin Devon believes that I would ever be his wife. However, my excitement quickly turned into loneliness as I remembered that Tanya, my only friend, had gone overseas for the summer right after graduation. I really missed having long conversations with her about everything, anything, and nothing at all.

Since I had nowhere else to put my feelings, I decided to write them down. I wrote a note for Trevor and another one to Devon just to get my true feelings out there. I wrote the letters and rewrote them a dozen times in my head before letting the pen touch the paper.

"Dear Trevor," no, how about *"Greetings Trevor Boo,"* no ok, *"Hey Trevor*, I hope this letter finds you in good health."

Wait, I sound like a school nurse, that's not going to work. As I tapped my pen against the blank paper, tiny marks began to form, and I stared at them, waiting for inspiration to strike. I rewrote the sentence repeatedly – at least ten times – until finally, the perfect words came to me. Aha!

Hey,
I wanted to take the time to say I really have a crush on you. Let me know if you like me too. Write back to me and let me know.
Yours Truly,
Jackie

"Hey" was the perfect opening, short, sweet and to the point, just like my note. I wanted to finally get beyond feeling so awkward around him, but, at the same time, not say too much and end up embarrassing myself. Now, it was time for Mr. Mint breath. I still could not believe his nerve! First, Devon embarrassed me in front of Trevor by calling me out and then he suddenly got all brave and forward, even pinning me against a gate to declare his love and stake his claim on me. Ugh! I closed my eyes and tried to shake off the disgusting image.

It was best to keep things simple with Devon as well. What's a nice way to say go fly a kite?

Hey,

I wanted to say that although you are a nice guy and all, I don't get that vibe from you. Maybe there is another girl out there for you, I hope you find her.

Sincerely,

Jackie

Satisfied with my notes, I reached for the two envelopes in front of me; one was addressed to Devon and the other to Trevor. Just as I was about to stuff the letters in, I heard my mother call, "Dinner time."

Mama! I fumbled with my papers as a thin layer of sweat covered my body. The last thing I wanted was for my mother to come in and find me writing letter to "man" as she called any male no matter how old, or young they were.

This moment reminds me of Dean. He is the reason that I almost had a coronary when I heard my mother approaching. Dean was a boy who had a schoolboy crush on me in junior high. He wrote me a note asking if I liked him with two checkboxes, one for *yes* and one for *no. Talk about simple!* But I was so embarrassed I didn't know what to do, so I stuffed his letter into the pocket of my school uniform. Well, was that ever a mistake! By the end of the school day, Dean's letter was forgotten, until that fateful day - laundry day.

It was raining. I remember because my socks were soaked and muddy from the puddles, I stepped in on my way home. My mother was standing in the kitchen near the door with her arms folded, tapping her toe and frowning.

"Good afternoon mama, how are you?" I asked, not sure what to make of her standing there glaring at me.

"Good afternoon nuh?" she hissed.

I knew something was up then because somehow her greeting sounded like fighting words. I stayed quiet trying to gauge what the issue was, the silence was deafening but I dared not to speak first.

"So, a dis me send you go to school fa?" she asked.

I knew that the way I answered this question could potentially detonate whatever threatened to explode behind my mother's gaze. It was particularly difficult to respond when she was this fired up, so I humbly repeated, "school?"

"Yes school, did I send you to school to look man!" she raged.

Now I was at a loss for words. I had no idea what she was talking about. I think the blank stare on my face enraged her more. I don't know why though, maybe she thought I was trying to be slick or something. It had already been a couple of days and I genuinely forgot all about the note that trouble-making Dean had given me.

Mama was growing impatient, and it became clear to her that she was getting nowhere with me. Finally, she shook out the wrinkled paper she had mangled in her grasp and slammed it on the table. My eyes burned as I squinted to identify what it was.

The note had new creases, but I recognized the handwriting—it was the note from Dean. Mama wasn't alone; I wanted to beat myself for making such a careless mistake.

"Is wah dis!" Mama demanded.

I wanted to pounce on that paper and tear it into a million pieces, but it was too late, the nasty mangy cat was already out the bag.

"A note," I replied, "Some boy in my class gave me that." There was nothing left to do but be honest, however; my confession seemed to dig an even deeper hole. "Some bwoy, inna class!" Mama's habit of repeating everything ten times louder than you originally said it had set in.

"Me send you aH school fe look man? Your father and I work haaaarrrrddddd to mek sure you get a good education and instead a study yuh booooook you a look MAN!"

Mama emphasized her words through wild gesticulations and projectile spitting when she was really upset. It wasn't intentional, but all her children were aware that when Mama got mad, for whatever the reason, just be prepared to be showered.

I was banished to my room without being able to tell the full story, at this point, I dared not protest. What was a thirteen-year-old to do?

I remember how she scandalized me over that note. When Dada came home, she embellished what happened adding extras to make it appear worse than it was. In her re-telling of story, I had become a junior high drop out *with belly!* Not to mention that everyone who called on the phone for the next week had to hear about "Jackie, man, and the note."

"Jackie, dinner I am calling you!"

I could hear her footsteps approaching my bedroom door, which was never allowed to be fully closed unless I was changing; this was another one of our infamous house rules. *Hurry Jackie hurry!* I grabbed the letters and stuffed each one quickly into the envelope I had prepared, then scanned my room urgently for a place to stash them. Without much time left, I settled for them between the pages of the dictionary laying on my bed.

Look normal, her shadow reflected on the wall as she pushed the door wide open. I turned over several pages of the thick dictionary and read the first word that caught my eye aloud.

"Homeostasis," I said feigning intrigue, "interesting word."

"Jackie, do you hear me calling you, what you in here doing?" Mama asked, then answered her own question, "Oh you are reading good. Well take a break and come to dinner."

The entire time she stood in the doorway, I held my breath and didn't exhale until I heard her footsteps fade down the hallway.

"Ok, mama I am just going to wash up, I'll be right there."

Dinner that night was sweet! My favorite was served—lamb chops, garlic mash potatoes and sautéed spinach. Dada and mama were at the table discussing the latest news as usual. I heard them saying that the adoption was almost complete, and they would soon have to go and sign the final paperwork. I sat quietly at the table; my thoughts were miles away obsessing over the letters I had written and trying to figure out how or when I could get them to Devon and Trevor.

CHAPTER SEVEN

The next morning, I awoke feeling completely wired. Torturing myself all night, listening to love songs, and playing out every possible scenario, I was a nervous wreck. But even more pressing was the problem of leaving the house. How could I ever have the chance to see him and confess my feelings if I couldn't even make it past the breakfast table?

My parents were up acting out their morning routines in the kitchen. *Ah, yes, the library!* You could practically see the light bulb go off when it came to me that asking to go to the library was my get out of jail free card. Recently, I had taken an interest in Middle Eastern culture and my parents knew that I wanted to research it further. I was sure that they would allow me to go out to the library because anything that had to do with learning was an automatic pass.

The two envelopes were still nestled in the dictionary, so I quickly sealed them before slipping them into my brand-new backpack, a thoughtful graduation present from my parents. It was the perfect accessory for my upcoming library adventure. On my way out the door, the phone rang, begrudgingly I turned back. Another unspoken rule in my house was that if the phone rang, while any of us children was near it, we were obligated to answer it, no matter what we were doing. So, I did.

"Hello, Brown residence."

The ecstatic voice on the other end made up for my lack of enthusiasm.

"Jackie!" she said calling out my name triumphantly.

"This time I got it right! It's your Auntie Dolores again. How you do?"

Her again, I scrunched my face and waited for the pleasantries to be over so that I could politely hand the phone over to mama. For reasons unbeknownst to me, this lady, who I absolutely have no recollection of, wanted to chit-chat with me first.

"Did your mother tell you?" she asked excitedly.

Parents can be fickle, always concerned about being embarrassed by misbehaving, unruly children. Mine were adversely opposed to the concept of a "pickney government", I couldn't afford for anything to go wrong so I decided to hold back any smart remarks. It took everything I had to answer nicely, in an appropriate little girl tone, so as not to sound *grown*.

No, she didn't." I responded after much deliberation, in a practiced kiddy tone.

"I am coming into town; we have a wedding reception to go to. Your mother told me she is busy and not in the mood to *go a road*, so she suggested I take you with me."

"Me?" I answered too quickly to hide how absurd this sounded.

What in the world? My parents went from having me under lock and key to allowing me to go out with some strange woman, who says she is my Auntie. I didn't have time to process this weird turn of events; I had a date with destiny. I mean the library. Nonetheless, I politely cut the conversation short and asked if she would like to speak with my mother.

"Mama," I called out before she could answer, "Auntie Dolores is on the phone."

I handed my mother the receiver and flung my bag over my shoulder then leaned in to kiss mama on her cheek. She waved me off and kept talking.

I did not want to lie about having been to the library, so I had limited time to swing by Trevor and Devon's block and pray that they were out on the stoop or something. What was I going to say? Should I just hand them the letters? Should I say something or just smile? I stood in front of my building for about five minutes trying to figure out the best strategy. Just as I was deliberating the wildest thing happened, I saw Devon walking up my block. Again! What is he doing over here? Familiar butterflies immediately began fluttering wildly from my belly into my chest.

There was no doubt about it, Devon is becoming a wildcard. I did not want him to pull another stunt like he did the other day. I quickly walked off my stoop and headed in the opposite direction. I knew he would follow me, I was counting on it, this way I could lure him away from the watchful eyes and ears of my neighbors. As I crossed over Jefferson and 1st streets, I could hear Devon panting heavily behind me.

"Stop, Jackie, stop!"

I finally slowed down and turned around to face him.

"Oh, hey Devon how are you doing?" Prentending to see him for the first time.

"I know you saw me, girl why are you playing hard to get?" "You got a brother out here breathing heavy trying to run you down."

I resisted the urge to chuckle because the truth was that, as a friend, Devon was kind of cool. He always made me laugh and ever since we met in the sixth grade we got along. But only as friends, for some reason I didn't feel, well you know, "the vibe" for him.

At any rate, I liked the attention he gave me, confusing right, especially because I had a crazy crush on his cousin. *Don't judge me.*

"Jackie, I am going off to college early, taking some summer classes."

Oh no, what should I say? I needed to stop him before he tried to pull another stunt like he did the other day. I remembered the letters I had with me, one for him and one for Trevor. *Quick Jackie, say something!*

"Devon look, I have something for you."

"For me?"

"Yes,"

He watched with rapt attention as I rifled through my inner pocket to ensure I retrieved the one with his name on it.

"Voila," I beamed with pride, presenting it to him. He took the sealed envelope from my hand, inspecting it carefully and holding it up to the sun.

"Read it when you get home Devon, we can catch up some other time."

"I'm out," I exclaimed, darting away before he could protest.

"Phew, that was close!"

Devon was out of sight, and it was time to track down Trevor. I checked their block, but he wasn't there. *Perhaps he was playing basketball?* As I approached the courts, I noticed a group of guys playing a heated game of shirts and skins while a cheering squad of girls sat in the bleachers. He was nowhere in sight, so I decided to head to the library.

"Looking for someone?"

The voice was low and seasoned with spice. Fever sweat washed over me, and every muscle in my body froze. It suddenly occurred to me that we'd never really spoken alone before. *Come on Jackie, be cool. Slowly,* I coached my legs to be steady, silently begging them not to collapse beneath me and turn with poise. *Oh, my goodness, my crush he spoke to me! Oh, that's right,* he did speak to me, didn't he? What do I do? What do I say? He'll think I am an idiot if I just stand here staring at him.

"Um hey, how are you?"

"I am good, just coming to shoot some hoops, what are you doing here?"

I couldn't say *stalking you,* so I came up with something that sounded less creepy.

"Well, you know, I was passing by."

It sounded awkward; yet it was plausible, so I went with it.

"It's a good thing I bumped into you."

"Really, why?"

"Because, I have something for you."

"For me?" he asked. They were the same words that his cousin had spoken just a few minutes earlier, but they felt so different. Trevor didn't seem excited, just confused.

"Yeh, I wrote you something." I said fishing through my bag and retrieving the remaining envelope with Trevor's name on it.

"Hoped to see hear from him soon."

"I flashed him a toothy smile before he waved and walked away."

Ahhhhh! I want to scream, jump, flip and do the moonwalk all at the same time. *Me seh me glad bag did buss!*

When I finally got to the library, I hastily checked out a few books on the Mediterranean and made my way home. This was the best day I've had since, well ever! I was too hyped nothing could bring me down. As I entered the house, mama was getting dinner on the table and dada was listening to the nightly news. My brothers were home from classes and playing their music loudly in the back. At dinner, everyone was sharing how their day went, and dada noticed I was in a great mood.

"A wah sweet yu so princess?" he asked.

"Oh, I just had a great day, that's all."

"Well, I am glad you feel good," said mama, "because after dinner you must fit the dress I have been working on. Your Auntie Dolores is coming up from back home and you will be accompanying her to a wedding reception this Sunday coming."

"Sunday coming? Is anyone coming with me, I don't even remember this woman."

"No, we can't make it, but we want you to go and bring our congratulations to the family. They used to be our neighbors back home."

"Dada, why can't you come?"

"I have to work overtime that day, and your mother is not up to it."

"What about the boys?" I asked, grasping at any hope that I wouldn't have to go or at least not go alone!

"They already have plans, and it was short notice."

So, there it went—my good mood, usurped by some strange person's wedding, and an estranged Auntie from back home.

"I want you to be on your best behavior," my mother warned.

"Yes mama." I promised.

"I want you to remember to say please and thank you," she lectured.

"Yes mama," I repeated.

"I want you to stay close to Dolores and don't wander off wid people you don't know," Mama said as though she was completely unaware of the irony in her statement.

Really, like this strange woman? How many times had I said that I didn't know this Auntie Dolores person, but I dared not say that aloud, so instead I mumbled, "Yes mama."

After dinner, my mother and I headed straight for her bedroom. "Try on this." She said handing me a dress made from the fabric my father had bought for me a while ago. My mother was an exceptional seamstress. She designed my dress with a train, bolero, and matching head wrap. I didn't know who else was going to be there, but I did know I was going to be stepping in *ready fe de video light.*

CHAPTER EIGHT

Sunday came quickly. The doorbell rang followed by several minutes of loud laughter and commotion at the entrance before mama emerged with a tall slim woman. She rushed towards me and pulled me into her bosom hugging me tightly.

"You nuh memba me?" she asked pushing me away so that I could get a good look at her.

"Oh, my goodness, Priscilla you nuh see how you last daughter get so big."

Priscilla was my mother's name; mama wasn't big on having friends either, so we hardly ever heard anyone call her by her name these days.

"Yes, she is getting ready to start City College this fall."

"Wow," Auntie Dolores said nodding approvingly before getting right to the reason for her visit.

"You ready?"

"Not yet," I said as I scurried back to my room to finish getting dressed. As I did, I could hear them two catching up on old times and news from back home.

I'd been sheltered for so long; I was nervous about going out to such a big event without my parents.

"Come Jackie, let me take your picture so your father can see." Mama waved me over to where she waited with Auntie Delores.

I posed, taking several pictures, Mama even let me sit in her "living room," you know the one room in the house that no one is allowed to go into. I started to feel grown, especially since children were not allowed in here. The mood was festive, and I started to think that maybe the night wouldn't be so bad after all. We said our goodbyes to mama and made our way to the car where Auntie Dolores had a driver waiting. As we pulled off, she launched right into conversation.

"So, you have boyfriend?" she asked, tilting her head as if to see my expression better.

My eyes bulged out of my head; as you know, divulging this type of intel to parental friendly adults is a *no, no*. I just stared at her. She laughed.

"Girl please me did young one time too," Auntie Dolores gently slapped me on the leg closest to her.

"I know your mother, she kinda ol fashion; but you don't have to worry about me tonight. I come to get my groove on and have some fun. Just mek sure I can find you when it's time to go."

She pushed up her bosom in her bra to perk them up a bit, after which she pulled out her contact mirror to reapply some lipstick. I watched as she gave herself a wink and then snapped it shut. *What? Is this woman for real? She intends on leaving me unattended!* I tried to remain calm and not to let on how alarmed I was for the rest of the ride. After about twenty minutes, we arrived at the wedding hall in Brooklyn. Reggae and calypso music streamed out the doors every time someone entered or exited. There were many men and women all dressed up in flashy sequin gowns, linen suits, flashy gold jewelry, and fanciful hairdos.

My eyes were full to the brim with the vibrant array of characters in attendance; I thought to myself, *I am in for a good night.* Auntie Dolores walked me in and introduced me to a few people. Every introduction went something like this, *"You nuh memba Priscilla and her husband, the ones who did leave the island and come ah foreign. You remember them man, dem used to live inna de green house with the orange veranda at the top of the lane. The husband used to work up a di factory."*

Then the person would have the vague, confused look until suddenly a light bulb moment occurred, *"Oh yes man me memba dem. Well, this is Jackie dem last daughter."*

Each and every time Auntie Dolores finally got around to saying who I was, they followed with, *"Wow she grow big eh."*

Anyway, that is pretty much how the night began, Auntie Dolores said she was going to the bar and asked if I wanted something to drink. I wondered if she was already drunk to be asking me about alcohol, just in case, I made a point of requesting juice. She came back with two cups; she handed me a punch cup and said to drink up.

Alone in a room full of strangers, I resorted to one of my favorite pastimes, people watching. I couldn't help but notice who was intoxicated, who was eating all the food, and who loved to dance. After being missing for over an hour, I decided to check on my Auntie Dolores. The punch she made for me was finished, and I felt a bit lightheaded. Although I wasn't sure why, I guessed that I was probably just hungry. My parents often warned me about *nyaming a road* so I was apprehensive about eating the food served at the reception, but I decided that on my way back from the bathroom, I would get more of that delicious fruit punch.

On my way back I saw two young men approaching. They looked oddly familiar, but the dim lighting over the dance floor made it difficult to make out their faces. As they came closer, a strobe light shone, and a side of their faces was highlighted. With excitement, I squealed; it was Trevor and Devon!

Quick, look natural... no check to make sure you look alright. Now was my chance, Trevor and I could talk all about how he was checking for me too and how he had just as much of a crush on me as I did on him. From a near distance, I saw Devon whispering to Trevor. I watched as Trevor looked my way and waved his hand dismissively.

Huh? What was that about?

Lost in a moment of distress I didn't notice that Devon continued to advance toward me smiling, no smiling is an understatement; he was cheesing from ear to ear. He offered himself a seat and proceeded to inch up very close to my right leg.

"What's up Jackieee, my love?"

I was too disoriented to focus. He leaned in resting his hand on his jaw and just stared at me. The burning sensation of his laser beam stare snapped me back to my senses and forced me to assess my current situation. Something was going on and I needed to find out what was up.

"Hey Devon,"

"Surprised to see you here."

"Yeh my family knows the couple who got married."

"Small world."

"Yeh, small world indeed," I retorted.

I half-heartedly spoke to Devon as I watched intently to see where Trevor went next; it was frustrating because he kept slipping out of sight.

"Um, Devon."

"Yes babes" he answered, prepared to grant whatever I asked for next.

"Can you watch my purse for a minute?" I asked.

Wait, why did he call me babes? I couldn't stop to rebuke him; I needed to speak to Trevor first. I could always come back and straighten Devon out after.

"No worries sweets," I heard Devon reply obligingly, as I walked away in search of his cousin, "I will be right here when you get back."

Finding Trevor was a priority, but suddenly I had a more pressing issue. My bladder made demands overriding my heart and forced me off to the lady's room. As surprised as I was to be making my second trip to the bathroom so soon, I was stunned by what I saw in the hallway when I was done. You wouldn't believe who I saw pressed up against some girl wearing a cocked off ponytail and what looked like only half of a gown probably meant for her little sister.

You guessed it, *Trevor.*

Is this what he thought of my note? Was this his answer? Should I say something to him, or just walk away?

He was smiling and whispering into her ear. I could not help but stare at them. So many questions were swimming around in my mind. I had never seen this girl before; she is not from our school or our neighborhood. None of that mattered now and what happened next, I was certainly not prepared for. Trevor caught me staring at him in disbelief and just as we made eye contact, he went in for a big passionate kiss. He initiated it, I saw him; she was there playing with the collar on his button down charcoal grey shirt, and he was there stroking the strands of her lopsided ponytail. As soon as he saw me come out of the bathroom, he cut his eyes at me. Then, right there for everyone to see, he put his lips right on his *hallway jubie.* Their heads started moving back and forth. I could not believe my crush was playing kissy face in the hallway right in front of me.

This must be why they called it a crush; people get hurt. Trevor had shatterd my perfect image of him. I hung my head and walked back to the table where Devon was sitting. As I approached him, I could see the gleam of his perfectly aligned teeth shining in the dimly lit room. He was bubbling and excited, but I was too disappointed to ask him about what. He started talking and I was in no mood to scold him, my heart was too heavy, so I let him prattle on uninterrupted.

"I knew you were the one, ever since I first laid eyes on you."

"I am glad you finally came around."

"Jackie," he reached for my hand put it into his and looked deeply and longingly into my eyes.

"I can't wait to come and ask your parents for permission to marry you."

My ears were listening to Devon, but my eyes were glued on Trevor and *Ponytail girl* who decided to bring their show to the dance floor.

"Married," I repeated still in a trance and only half listening,

"What are you talking about Devon?"

"The note Jackie, the one you gave me the other day about you having a crush on me. I have told you for years that I want more that a school yard affair; girl I am going to make you, my wife."

"What note Devon?

"Oh, the note… WAIT WHICH NOTE!"

Shock and dismay washed over me as I realized that I had given Trevor the wrong note and now Devon thinks I want to be with him. Sweaty. My palms began to sweat profusely; the shock was too much to bear. What was I going to do, what could I say?

Trevor and his hallway girlfriend were on the dance floor when suddenly the music switched to one of my favorite lover's rock song. They danced slowly before me; he was rocking away as she lost herself in his embrace. There was nothing I could do; I felt my heart burning inside. They started to do a provocative looking slow whine that was way too advanced for me.

"Jackie, come let's dance." I heard Devon say.

I was upset, embarrassed and didn't want Trevor to think he got one over on me, so I accepted.

Devon was the perfect gentleman; he held my hand and danced slow. He looked at me lovingly, he kept a safe distance and didn't try and touch my behind or anything. For the first time in the most confusing moment in my life, I saw Devon differently. I don't know what it was, maybe the punch, maybe I was hurting, or maybe he really was a good guy, all I knew was at that moment, just for that moment, I forgot about everything.

After the dance, Devon escorted me back to the table and said he had to make rounds greeting everyone, but he would be back soon. Auntie Dolores finally reappeared after being missing for hours; she claimed that she came to check on me and make sure I was having a good time. I was far from having a good time and was so ready to leave.

"I hope you not ready yet," she shouted above the music, "because I'm not."

She wasn't kidding, her bangs were pasted to her forehead with sweat and the nice sequin high heel shoes she wore coming, were now in her hands. She sat for a moment rubbing her bunions and smiling at a man in an orange suit. As soon as the song changed again, she boogied, barefooted, right back towards the dance floor.

Devon returned not too long after, just as he said he would. He stayed and we spoke for most of the night. He told me about his plans for college and what he planned to study; he asked about my family and what I wanted to become after school. As we spoke, there were times that I could see his cousin Trevor through my peripheral vision signaling to him that he was ready to go. I never turned to look at Trevor directly, but I was able to make out him waving his hand and pointing to his watch impatiently. But Devon kept waving him off, determined to make his time with me last if only to learn about or share one more detail with me. Eventually, Trevor grew impatient enough to walk over to where we were sitting.

"Cuz, I don't want to break up your little date, but it is time to go."

Devon had driven there, and he didn't want it to be a problem, so he elected to pull the car around. As he waited, Trevor stood at a close distance with his back turned. *Should I speak or should I wait for him to speak to me?* I decided I didn't have much time until Devon came back. My curiosity rose and I just had to find out what Trevor was thinking after this mix up.

"Did you get my note?" I asked, I wanted to tap his shoulder, but I didn't.

"Yes, and as you can see I "found me a girl that's right for me,'" he replied coldly spitting the words I'd written in the note back at me.

"Ah, let me explain I ..., wait..." I stammered.

"No, you wait, I didn't approach you, you were the one always looking at me and when you finally have something to say, you write to reject me."

"But I see you have been all buddy, buddy with my cousin now; he is the better man for you anyways, because to be my girl, you have to put out!"

"Put out," even as I repeated the words, I wasn't sure what he meant by them.

I didn't have enough time to ask.

Trevor made sure to rub in how attractive he found *Ponytail Girl* and emphasized every curve of her body energetically then announced that because she was his type, he would be dating her. I was flabbergasted; I was completely speechless anyway, so I let him vent. He was truly upset and continued a rant that went between how sexy that girl was and how rude I was for writing that letter to him; I never got the chance to say that he got the wrong note. To be honest, I wasn't sure that he had anymore.

Trevor stormed off towards the door, pushing past Devon, who had just returned from bringing his car around; I just sat there watching him. Suddenly, Devon stood in front of me filling my gaze and blocking my view of Trevor. He was saying something about seeing me again and meeting my parents before he left for college the next week. I tried to focus on what he was telling me but at that point everything was just too much. *My parents?* I had already had enough excitement for the night, and I would have to cross that bridge when I got to it.

Devon reached out for a hug and for the first time, I let him hug me. His arms were so warm and inviting, I found comfort there until I remembered where I was. We were surrounded by adults, who while seeming to be about their own business of enjoying the festivities were perfectly capable of mentally recording every detail and reporting back to my parents what they had seen and what they thought about it. I found my way back to my station as I called it and a few minutes later, Auntie Dolores reappeared in a huff saying she was ready to go. She seemed agitated. I didn't ask and she didn't tell.

I got home and my parents had already gone to bed. I couldn't sleep that night. I went to my room and replayed the entire night. Despite being disappointed about Trevor, Devon managed to pique my interest and suddenly became more attractive.

Wednesday came and I hadn't seen or heard anything from Devon since the reception on Sunday. I began to wonder if he had been serious about talking to my parents. My mother made oxtails, rice and peas, fried plantains with garden salad for dinner that night, which happened to be another one of my favorite meals. As I prepared to set the table for dinner, the doorbell rang; smiling, my father asked me to answer it. I opened the door to find Devon standing there with a bouquet of flowers.

"Devon what are you doing here?" I asked, not able to believe that he really came.

"I am here to speak with your parents, my love."

Is he kidding? The dizziness had finally subsided and to be honest I spent the last three days just trying to figure out what really happened between us. Devon explained that during that time, he told his parents about his intention and that his parents called my parents. The adults spoke on the phone at length about his intentions to marry me and ultimately agreed to him discussing it with them over dinner tonight!

What kind of madness is this? I thought to myself. Had graduating high school unlocked yet another unexpected rite of passage into womanhood? "Looking man" had always been considered a curse word, and the mere mention of one could land me in hot water. Yet, there I was, inviting a *man* into my home to share a meal at the same table where my dad drank his cinnamon tea and read the paper in the morning. I wasn't sure what would come next, but I could see him patiently waiting for my invitation in the doorway.

Apprehensively, I stepped to the side and gestured for him to come inside. I could smell his cologne as he passed, his shoes were shining, and from head to toe, there wasn't a spot or wrinkle on him. He could not stop smiling the entire night and for the first time, since I've known him, I was the one in awe.

Can you believe dada and mama took to Devon right away? They were warm, inviting and surprisingly receptive to the idea of us getting married sometime in the future. Devon told them that he knew he loved me for a very long time and said that until now I played hard to get and made things difficult for him. I couldn't stop looking at him, he was amazing, and he seemed to have won my parents over so easily with his charm. *How did I miss it?* I listened as my parents gave him hard-earned praise saying that they could tell that he came from good parenting, that his family had a good reputation in the community and that they would love to have him as a son-in-law some day.

Devon assured my parents that he planned to attend college first and only after graduating would he return to claim me as his bride. I didn't say much, and I don't remember being asked much either. Once dinner was over, I asked Devon if we could go out to the front porch and talk. He seemed eager to have a moment alone with me and agreed.

We stood outside. *This is different,* I thought.

"Why so quiet Jackie?" Devon asked.

I didn't know how to start the conversation; I wasn't even sure if I wanted to confess the truth about the note at all.

"Jackie, do you know I really love you with all my heart."

"I want to give you the world, make you happy, and never cause you pain."

He sounded so sincere; plus, my parents loved him. I could not bring myself to tell him about the note. It didn't matter now, I tried to tell myself.

"I'm leaving this Sunday to start the summer semester, I am going to become an architect and when I am done, I am going to make you, my wife. The school is only upstate so we can stay in touch. I will be back often; please promise you will write and call me."

Devon sounded so confident while speaking about his plans, but his voice weakened as he sought my assurance that I would write and call while he was away. All I could do was muster up a smile. That was enough. He took that as my agreement and left.

-~-

Over the next four years, Devon studied to be an architect and I studied to become a writer. Before we knew it, college graduation was around the corner and after graduation meant wedding. When the time came, I attended Devon's graduation with my family and his family joined him when he attended mine. They began to bond as prospective in-laws, and everyone looked forward to the big day.

Was I ready to get married? I had grown to love Devon and we promised each other we would wait until we were married to become intimate. Surprisingly, we kept that promise. He proved he was everything that I needed, but I still wasn't sure if I was ready to be a wife.

I had long put Trevor out of my mind especially after I heard he ended up doing time for aggravated assault. Ponytail Girl, who I later found out was really named Pam, ended up becoming his baby mama, and by the time we finished undergrad, he had two children with her and one on the way. It was hard for Trevor to get a good paying job and the last I heard, he hung out at the liquor store all day, rolling dice, and chanting reggae lyrics.

Chapter Nine

The inheritance from Mr. Carleton changed everything. We started arranging the actual wedding right after our unexpected win fall. It was a relief to know that we didn't have to worry about money and that we had inherited a place to live. No rent or mortgage, debt free baby! We were set for the next ten years but in the meantime, we had to stay at our respective parents' house until the wedding.

One day, Devon called me saying that the lawyer's office called again, he was already out on that side of town so we agreed he should go alone. *Fine with me, I thought.* I was busy in my room thumbing through wedding catalogs and planning our big day.

-~-

What could Mr. Thompson possibly want? He arrived just after lunchtime and as he was about to press the buzzer, he noticed that the door wasn't fully closed. Devon didn't think much of it and pushed it open to enter the building. The hallway leading to the lawyer's office was dimly lit and once outside the lawyer's door, he paused before knocking. Something felt strange. He began to rethink coming here without Jackie; she may not be overly friendly, but he thought she was a good judge of character. He contemplated whether he should go in or come back later. Just as he was about to turn around, he heard Rita's voice beckon him inside.

"Come in…"

Why was she purring like a cat, and why are the lights in here so dim? Devon stepped through the door and looked around, but he saw no one at the desk. He was certain he heard a voice say come in. This was odd, more than just odd, it was suspicious.

"Hello anybody here?" he inquired.

"Hello? Mr. Thompson, I am here, your secretary called me to talk about the estate."

There was an eerie silence and then Rita emerged closing the door behind him. Devon jumped back, startled by her behavior and uncertain of what she was up to.

"Devon," she purred again, "welcome back."

What's up with this woman and why does she sound like that?

Stuttering, nervously he asked, "Where, is Mr. Thompson?"

"Him not here, I was the one who called you." she confessed shamelessly.

Every fiber in his being told him this was not a good thing and that he should leave.

Rita was dressed in an above the knee hot red 'tight up' mini skirt, with matching v-neck, low cut, see-through blouse, and a black blazer.

"Where are your clothes?" he asked.

By now, Devon felt full court pressure; it was hard to look away as she had blocked his path. She laughed seductively, "Oh so you noticed. I knew you would like my new outfit."

She continued, "Look, I know you want me, I can see it in your eyes."

Want you, he mouthed disgusted by the thought.

Devon backed up as she advanced towards him; the space was small, she had him cornered, he stumbled over her desk while trying to get away.

The phone that was in his front pocket accidentally dialed; Jackie answered on the second ring.

"Hello, hello..." she said.

There was no answer on Devon's end, but she could hear rustling.

"Devon," Rita called again, "come to me I have some files for you to look over."

Jackie's heart skipped several beats, was she hearing what she thought she was hearing? Which woman dared speak to her fiance in this manner? She was tempted to hang up but decided against it; she wanted to hear Devon's response.

"Rita, I demand to know what this is about!" Devon said firmly.

"Where is Mr. Thompson?"

"Well since you don't want to play," Rita pouted,

"I guess I will just come out with it."

"I like and want to be with you," she proclaimed boldly.

"I can be a better wife than that Jackie you intend to marry." *WHAT!*

Devon was insulted; apparently Rita didn't know how much he loved Jackie and how long he'd planned to make her his wife.

"Rita, have you lost your mind?"

Each word flew like daggers across the room at her.

"Come on Devon," Rita said, clearly not registering how upset Devon was.

"I saw the way you were watching me when you came in here the other day. I saw her too unnu nuh match." Her heavily made-up face scrunched in disapproval.

"You want a woman like me who a go sweet you up baby."

"Me know how fe cook, clean and I can all tun night nurse when you need me."

Rita. Jackie heard her name and realized it was the rude front desk woman from the lawyer's office.

"Ma'am," Devon objected, intentionally using a formal tone to convey the distance he wanted to establish.

"I have no interest in you, and what you are doing is highly unprofessional."

Jackie smiled to herself and continued to listen.

"Devon stop playing hard to get, if me and you married, I can help you to get the monies from the will much faster and we can live life baby."

Rita tried to sound tempting as she ran her eyes down the length of his body.

"Oh," exclaimed Devon in a moment of clarity, realizing that all of this was really about Mr. Carleton's estate.

"I am not interested in you," he repeated.

"So please, if there is no further business today, I must go."

He headed towards the door. Rita rushed past him and slid between him and his escape. She blocked his way leaning forward and pushed her breasts up against him. As he struggled to avoid touching her, she took the opportunity to slap and grab his behind while drawing his pelvis towards hers.

"Tek your hands offa me woman, you mad or something!"

"Oh, Devon you are so attractive when you are mad."

"Say it again please," she said she asked, fluttering her fake lashes in a charming manner.

"Lady I am going to report you," he threatened.

"Ahhhh haaaa," she laughed almost maniacally.

"Report me, to whom, might I ask?"

"To your boss, Mr. Thompson," he shouted.

"My boss?" Rita said feigning brief confusion.

"You mean my dad, Mr. Thompson?"

"Your dad!" Devon repeated, completely taken aback. What kind of madness was this?

"Don't worry baby we have plenty of time for you to get all the details." Rita traced a line down his chest with one of her long, manicured fingers. Just then the office phone rang. Saved by the bell, she abruptly abandoned her seduction, to do her job and answer the phone.

"Stay right here baby I soon come back." She said while winking and walking away. She was sure that he was watching her ample bottom as she leaned over and stretched to pick up the receiver. Devon made his way to the door and turned the key left in its lock and sprinted down the hallway. Rita smirked as she watched him get away.

"He will be back, memba dat," she predicted confidently.

"That woman is off her rocker," Devon thought as he walked briskly down the street. *What type of people did Mr. Carleton leave to govern his estate? The lawyer is her father; what are they up to? Can you believe she tried to throw herself on me? What if Jackie was to find out and think that I wanted someone else.*

Absolutely not!

Devon shook off the idea of an impending scandal. He contemplated whether it was best to tell his fiancé or make sure that she never found out. He really did not have anyone to talk to about this. Mr. Carleton was dead, and his cousin Trevor had been trying to convince Devon that "something wasn't right," about Jackie and he should keep a good eye on her. Neither of the cousins told the other that they had received a letter from Jackie four years ago. Trevor had no idea that he received the hurtful words meant for Devon, and believing that they were her feelings towards him, he couldn't stand the mention of her name.

Devon called to check on Jackie as soon as he got home. He decided against telling her about the incident at the lawyer's office, but he really wanted to hear her voice. Jackie anticipated his confession during the entire call, but it never came. After that day, things changed in their relationship. Jackie was torn. She knew that Devon defended her and their relationship but at the same time, it didn't feel good that he never told her.

The next meeting to see the lawyer was scheduled for the following Thursday and Jackie contemplated confronting, "the likkle fast gal Rita." She felt unhinged and was desperate to talk to someone. That weekend, her oldest sister Tamar, came home to visit. This was the married sister, happily or not, Jackie needed to talk to someone, though she wasn't sure how much good advice she could expect. Tamar listened and told her to just wait; in her opinion, giving Devon some time to tell her on his own was better than making a scene.

"Just be glad he didn't give you bun," she said with a chuckle.
"Devon is a good man, not all of us are that blessed."

Chapter Ten

Mr. Thompson called again and advised Devon to stop in ASAP. It was raining that Thursday morning and Devon went through extra lengths this time to make sure he was personally in the office before he arrived for his appointment. The wedding date was set, and he figured their lawyer probably wanted to get started on the paperwork to release the first disbursement from Mr. Carleton's will. Jackie resolved that she would not let Devon go there alone anymore. She insisted that she got bad "vibes" from their office and wanted to come along as backup. Devon gave her no resistance on the matter. When they arrived at Mr. Thompson's office, things appeared to be in order. Rita was at the front desk this time in more suitable attire.

"Good morning, Devon," she said beaming.

"Oh, hey Jackie," she said, treating her like the little sister that tagged along.

Every bone in Jackie's body wanted to let her have it. *No Jackie just be cool everything will be alright. We are here to work out our wedding monies and investments. She is not worth it; Devon is your man, and he doesn't want her.*

Mr. Thompson was at the door. He waved them in and invited them to sit down.

"Let's cut to the chase!" Basil Thompson slapped his hands together as he sat.

"The other day, I forgot to read you one of the stipulations in the will."

I knew this man was shifty; this was too good to be true.

"What is the stipulation?" Devon asked.

"Well, there is this one little thing," the lawyer said pausing to build suspense, "Apparently Mr. Carleton only wants you to marry Jackie and if for any reason the marriage is called off you forfeit everything, the house, the monies... everything." Having said everything he wanted to say, he smiled and called Rita to escort them out.

"Rita dear, show my clients to the door please."

Jackie stood up to leave first and Devon followed behind her, Rita made her way towards them, she stopped behind Devon and gently squeezed his rear again. She then discreetly slipped a note into his back pocket.

Devon was frozen with anger and fear; he didn't want to alarm Jackie, so he acted as if nothing happened. A scandal would compromise his future home and wife. Once outside, Jackie noticed extra deep ridges that appeared on Devon's forehead. He was visibly upset.

"Baby, what's wrong?" Jackie asked, troubled by his expression. She assumed that he was worried about the new stipulation and sought to reassure him.

"We belong together that stipulation won't be a problem. Look at how long we have been planning to marry, even before we found out about the will."

"I know babes," Devon said, "but something doesn't feel right about this whole matter. I don't trust Mr. Thompson, or his secretary Rita."

Something was fishy about them, and he was looking for reassurance.

"Didn't you tell me that their vibe was off too?" He probed.

"Well yes, I find her to be very rude and crass, and him a bit unprofessional and untidy but what can we do? They are the ones Mr. Carleton left in change with what we need to get started on the right foot together. Let's just work on the wedding plans and get married as soon as we can."

Jackie was right.

They agreed that whatever those two were up to they needed to stay on their toes and move fast. Devon came home and undressed. He took off his pants and went through the pockets as usual before placing them in the dirty clothes hamper. During the routine search, he discovered Rita's letter. It reeked of cheap eau de toilette (toilet water) perfume.

> *Dear Devon,*
>
> *The other day was the best. I know you are playing hard to get, but I know you want me too. Together we can make the best couple. Yu fe dash weh dat all boring dry foot gal Jackie. I can make your life full of excitement. I was trying to tell you the other day that Mr. Thompson is my father. If me and you married trust me babes, we set for life. Oh, I'm not going to keep running you down so if you decided to marry Jackie, just know that I will have to tell daddy dearest and your beloved Jackie that you tried to "feel me up" the other day in the office.*
>
> *Talk Soon,*
>
> *Rita*
>
> *A dark red imprint of her full lips stained the signature line.*

I can't believe Rita is trying to blackmail me into leaving Jackie and marrying her. Man, I knew I should have told Jackie about what happened the other day. Now things are getting worse.

Everyone had already begun to work together in finalizing the details for their much-anticipated wedding. All the invitations were in the mail including, after much deliberation, one for Mr. Thompson and Rita.

Jackie's dress was custom designed by Mama who worked for weeks to finish every detail of the stunning gown. Mama was the seamstress for the entire wedding party. They decided to do away with convention complete with a costume change, after taking their vows clad in white, they'd change into royal garb as their reception attire. A regal purple trimmed with gold.

CHAPTER ELEVEN

The day of the wedding had finally arrived, both Devon and Jackie were nervous for more reasons than one. In Jackie's case, she knew that her veil was hiding more than just her face. How can I marry him and not tell him the truth? Some of their family members were not churchgoers, so they planned a non-traditional wedding. For the sake of peace, they agreed to rent a hall and allow a non-denominational layman to perform the ceremony.

The hall was beautiful. Crystal streamers fell elegantly from the ceilings like rain drops paused in mid-air; the windows were draped in shimmering lilac silk curtains that flowed in the light breeze. The chairs were wrapped in rich golden fabric and the aisles shimmered with the reflection of the golden ceiling. Exotic flowers towered on either side to create a breathtaking canopy. Everything seemed perfect.

Gasps of approval and admiration filled the quiet hall when Jackie appeared at the end of the long aisle.

It was everything Jackie dreamed of and more. Dada held her hand, grasping his youngest daughter tightly. "Calm down my princess, everything will be alright." His soft whisper was reassuring and filled her with a courage she lacked. But Jackie could not calm the uneasiness in her stomach; her hands began to perspire as was always the case when she was nervous.

Father and daughter slowly made their way down the aisle, Devon's cousin Sadie had an exquisite voice which swept through the hall as she sang Always and Forever. Devon was bubbling with anticipation; he stood in the front anxiously awaiting the moment he had been longing for. Ten years of dreaming, talking, and hoping that his one love would agree to marry him and by a twist of fate she did. No more waiting, the moment had finally arrived and just as the ceremony was about to get under way, a commotion could be heard stirring in the back of the hall.

The chatter from the crowd rolled in and increased loudly like locusts storming over fertile ground. Rita emerged from the shadows; she sauntered onto the bridal path and stood at the opposite end glaring at the couple with a villainous smirk. Suddenly, all eyes were on her, just as they should be as far as Rita was concerned. The atmosphere was filled with confusion, but one thing was for sure, Rita came to steal the show.

The group could be heard mumbling and jeering as she strolled purposefully down the aisle, her hips swayed in exaggerated seduction temporarily mesmerizing male guests who were pinched or popped by their female companions. She smiled obviously pleased with herself. From head to toe, Rita was a sight to behold. Her head was crowned with a cubic zirconia studded tiara; her voluminous body was stuffed in a skintight white dress that announced every curve, her long legs poured into sparkling red stilettos that boosted her height by six inches. Despite trying to appear confident, she could barely walk without stopping to balance every few steps. There was growing anticipation as the crowd's breath seemed to rise and fall with every step she took.

"Where is she going?"

"A who dis woman, and why is she here?"

Uneasy whispers swept through row after row of those that had gathered to see Jackie and Devon get married. It was hard for Jackie to see what the commotion was about; she squinted to make sense of the image approaching her. At first, she looked at

Devon, but he just shrugged his shoulders as it was hard for him to see that far down as well. After a few moments, as peering heads peeled back from the aisle and turned their gaze towards them, Jackie and Devon realized who it was.

Rita!

"Jackie," Devon whispered urgently, "we need a minute."

To the left of the canopy, there was a small room that was designated for the pastor to prepare before conducting the ceremony. Devon motioned to both of their parents that he needed a few minutes to speak with his bride. He grabbed Jackie firmly by the hand and escorted her to the room.

Calm down everyone, calm down bid the pastor, the couple will be back in a few minutes. Rita had finally arrived at her destination. Front row center. She used a narrow opening that was reserved for Jackie's older sister Tamar who was running late as usual. Rita rudely took a seat among the bride's' family.

"Scoot over nuh, me want fe see wah gwan."

"Who are you?" Mama demanded.

Jackie and Devon had made their way into a tiny room off the main hall. Inside the small room the air was thick with anticipation

"Sit down Jackie I have something to tell you."

Devon was terrified that Rita was going to ruin his wedding with lies and he could not hold this secret any longer. Jackie waited for months for Devon to trust her enough to confide in her about Rita. She had no idea he would wait right up until their wedding day. She was glad that he finally came around to telling her yet concerned that their marriage would be filled with secrets unless something drastic threatened to reveal it before they did.

"Jackie."

"Yes Devon."

"You know we have known each other for years."

"Yes Devon."

"Ever since I saw you in Ms. Margaret's 6th grade class, I knew you were the one for me."

"Yes Devon."

"For years, you never gave me the time of day, but I never gave up."

"Devon people are out there waiting."

"Let them wait, I have to get something off my chest."

"I knew for some time in high school you had a big crush on my cousin."

Oh, no! Jackie's heart began to beat faster. She wondered if he had found out about her little secret.

"I never knew what made you change your mind and give me that note, but since then my dream of having you as my wife has come true. I don't want anyone, anything, or any secret to come between us."

"I know Devon,"

Jackie was on the verge of breaking down; she feared how Devon would react if she told him that she had given him the wrong note. And that it was only after Trevor had rejected her that she decided to give him a chance.

He paused and took a deep breath.

"Jackie my love, I have something to tell you please don't get mad, please hear me out," he pleaded.

"A few months ago, when I went to the lawyer's office to clear up some paperwork," Devon began.

"Yeah," Jackie said wanting to give him the courage to continue.

"When I arrived, Mr. Thompson wasn't there." He blurted out.

"It was only Rita and Babes, you not going to believe this. The mad woman tried to throw herself on me. She said she wanted me to marry her instead of you."

"What!" Jackie had heard it all on the phone, but it still upset her to hear it again.

"Yes," Devon kept his head lowered looking only at Jackie's hands, which he was determined not to let go of, "but there is more. When I pushed her away and rejected her, she said if I didn't marry her that she would lie to you about it and tell Mr. Thompson that I assaulted her. I promise you I never touch the woman!"

Devon was looking into her eyes now; he needed her to believe him.

"I think that is why she came here today to cause a scene. I am sorry I took so long to tell you this." Devon braced himself for Jackie's reaction.

"Wow, Devon how could you hold something like this from me?" She said while chuckling lightly, which made Devon uncomfortable.

"Why are you laughing, how is this even funny to you?" Devon asked, genuinely perplexed.

"The truth is I already knew!" Jackie confessed, still smiling.

"What?" Devon asked, his expression was quizzical, his confusion begged for an explanation.

"When you went to the office that day, my phone rang. I could hear your conversation, and I heard her come on to you. I also heard you reject her. I was waiting for you to tell me about it, but you never did. What troubled me the most was how long you kept it from me."

Jackie suddenly realized how hypocritical she sounded.

"I'm so, so sorry Jackie." Devon said, placing two strong hands on her shoulders but unable to face her, "I thought maybe you wouldn't believe me or think that I really wanted Rita and did something to lead her on. I was wrong not to trust your love for me."

Her smile faded and quiet filled the room. She knew that it couldn't end here; hanging in the silence that followed Devon's confession was still one more secret, Jackie's.

Slowly lowering her head Jackie spoke softly, this time it was she that couldn't meet his gaze.

"Devon," she began.

"Yes Jackie..." Devon answered, like a sinner awaiting judgment.

"I have something to tell you as well."

What possibly could she have to say? He wondered.

"Well, I know I should have told you this long ago but," as Jackie continued her words echoed in his ears.

Backside, she cheat on me, no, she change her mind and don't want to marry me again. Devon mind cycled through scenarios each one worse than the last.

His face tensed up, his eyes searched hers, simultaneously demanding that she continue and praying that she wouldn't.

Jackie continued.

"I just didn't know how to say it."

Devon braced himself for the possibilities that flooded his imagination. He exploded anxiously saying, "Just get to it Jackie!"

"Remember, right before high school graduation, when I saw you that day and gave you a note." Jackie's words were still measured and cautious.

"If I remember? That was the note that changed everything," Devon said, nodded his head slightly, unable to make sense of how this could be related to Rita or the wedding.

"You finally realized that I was the better choice instead of my cousin."

Jackie's eyes widened as if they were taking in the magnitude of the situation. *Oh boy, how do I go on? What if he gets so upset that he wants to call off the wedding?* She continued choosing her words very carefully.

"The truth is…"

"Jackie come on nuh, can we reminisce on the honeymoon, people are outside waiting."

"Wait nuh, Devon this is hard enough as it is, please give me a minute to say it."

She lifted her pearl white veil and let it rest on her head.

"Jackie, what is the problem? You are starting to scare me now. What you give me bun?"

"No!"

"What? You don't want to marry me again?" Devon said, throwing out another one of his fears and hoping she would say no again.

"No, that's not it; I just can't hide this lie anymore."

Jackie cried.

Just then a knock came to the door. The pastor pushed his head in, "the people are waiting is everything good in here?"

"Yes, pastor all is well; we are coming just ironing out a few things before the big I do." Devon said trying to sound as if he believed his words.

"Ok, well, try and speed it up, the people are getting restless and hungry, and you know how that is. I don't know why dem love bring dem belly come a road," the pastor jested.

He closed the door, a strong wind passed through the room. Jackie fumbled over her words trying to figure out how to say what she needed to say. *Maybe I should leave well enough alone, she thought, but then another thought came saying no secrets in your marriage girl, just fess up.*

"Devon, like I was saying, I really, really, really have grown to love you." Jackie spoke quickly, she had to just get this over with, "I always considered you my friend and I am grateful of the opportunity to consider you, my husband."

"And?"

"Well, the note, the note I gave you that day was um... it was actually not for you." She blurted out and cringed as she waited for his response. Devon twisted his mouth confused because Jackie wasn't making any sense.

"What do you mean?" he asked.

"I mean, I wrote two notes back then, one for you and one for Trevor, I accidently gave Trevor your note and you got Trevor's note." Jackie explained.

"I had such a crush on him, and I wanted to let him know but you were always there embarrassing me, so I decided to tell him in a note. Your note said that I think you should go find another girl, because I was not the one for you."

The people outside were getting restless. Fortunately, Sadie was called to sing another song; the pastor was working hard to keep the crowd at bay.

Devon was crushed; he knew that something must have happened to change Jackie's mind, but he never thought in a million years that that it was an accident!

"So, are you saying you just got stuck with me by default? That you really didn't want to be with me? And I was an accident?" Devon fumed.

"No, no baby, well yes and no." Jackie had never seen Devon this angry, at least not with her.

"Please just listen." Jackie asked hoping that she could deescalate the situation. "It was providence. I didn't know what I needed; I was just an immature girl at the time with a high school crush. The Creator knew that we were supposed to be together. He knew that you were the man I needed."

Devon arose from his seat with a grimace on his face. He turned his back so that she could not see the pain gripping his heart.

"Why did you keep this from me so long?" He asked. "Why are you telling me this on our wedding day?"

"I want us to be honest with each other." Jackie answered.

Devon thoughts turned to Rita's words that day at the office. Was she right, was she the better woman to be his wife? He had invested so much in building a solid foundation, how could he reconcile that with how he felt right now. He made his way towards the door without saying a word. Jackie trembled with uncertainty. What was he doing, why is he not speaking.

Rita sat smugly in the front row reasoning that the delay meant victory for her.

A so me hot, as me come wedding stop.

CHAPTER TWELVE

Despite the bride's family protest, Rita refused to move until Devon came back. When Devon returned, he took his place in front of the guests, who had been impatiently waiting and requested a microphone. Jackie stood trembling standing off at a distance, anxiously awaiting his next move. Her fiancé took the microphone in hand and addressed the crowd in a stern voice.

"Attention everyone, attention I want to thank you for your patience and your attendance." Devon said, sounding clear and steady.

"Please listen up I have an announcement to make."

Announcement, what was he going to say?

Why wasn't Jackie standing with him?

The crowd started to whisper amongst themselves again in confusion.

"Please allow me to introduce someone to you."

Devon looked to the front and motioned to Rita to come up and join him. Rita could not believe this was really happening. She looked around for Jackie, but she was still hiding behind the wall watching everything play out. Rita adjusted her tiara and tugged at her dress, which had raised high along her thighs from sitting. She turned to the crowd with a smile and gave them a pageant wave.

Finally, a me name beauty queen. Look how everybody ah watch me, she reassured herself she was the prize winner. Once in front, Rita had a clear view of Jackie in the corner; she winked at her and mouthed *me have you man now.*

With a look of accomplishment still on her face, she turned her attention to her handsome catch, Devon. Devon's hand was extended towards her; she took it and together they faced the crowd.

"Elders, parents, family and friends, I am sorry for the delay on this special day, but an urgent matter came up that needed to be taken care of." He said addressing the crowd, "Jackie and I had a moment to reveal some secrets we were keeping and in the spirit of truthfulness, this is something I have to do."

Where was Jackie? Dada and mama had a despairing look on their faces. All of Jackie's siblings were troubled by the fact that another woman stood next to her husband to be on her wedding day. Her brothers were prepared for things to get ugly if they didn't see their baby sister soon.

"Everyone, I would like you to introduce you all to Rita."

Rita could barely contain her excitement. Mr. Thompson was in the back as giddy as a schoolboy. *Yes, Rita you did it, we inna de money now*, the lawyer rejoiced.

"Rita is a woman I met some time ago." Devon's voice echoed throughout the banquet hall, "She has shown me something special that I would like to share with you all."

"She showed me how much I," Devon looked back at Jackie as he continued, "How much I am worth having someone who loves me for me."

Rita smiled now that she had his heart she wondered if she should just marry Devon right now, there was already a Pastor and everything. She could always have a real wedding after she had all of Devon's money too. Jackie could not hold herself back anymore. She ran up to Devon, took his hand and began to profess her love in front of everyone.

"Devon, I do love you for you, I am sorry for not telling you sooner."

Now there were two women standing before the crowd.

"What kind of shame and disgrace is this," Auntie Dolores shouted out from the back row.

"I love you so much Jackie, but I."

"I have always loved you, but it hurts me to know you settled for your second choice."

"Devon, I grew to love you so much, I couldn't believe that I never saw how much we were meant for each other. I am sorry I kept that from you."

"Kept what!" one ol man in the back shouted.

"This sweeter than soap opera," another chimed.

"Devon don't do this!" Jackie pleaded.

"You kept a secret from me as well, for the same reason, you were afraid of how I would feel."

Rita realized her moment was short lived. She started to panic. She wedged her way between the couple as they drew closer together with each word.

"Devon, will you tell them, or should I?" Rita threatened desperately.

Just then Jackie extended her hand. Rita was unsure if she was reaching for Devon or if she planned to attack her but to her surprise, she took the microphone and stepped forward.

Standing where Devon had been, Jackie faced the audience and revealed that she knew all about Rita trying to seduce her man, Devon. When she finished, Jackie turned to face Rita, her expression was firm but no longer angry.

"I heard the whole thing," she told the stunned Rita, whose eyes darted nervously across the disapproving faces of the guests, "so please take your hands off of my fiancé and leave."

Rita looked down at her hand, her fingers still coiled tightly around Devon's wrist. All eyes were on Rita, and the weight of their judgment bore down on her like a ton of bricks. The label of homewrecker was now hers to bear, and she felt the heat of embarrassment flush her cheeks. Even her father had turned his back on her, leaving her to face the consequences alone.

She took a few paces backward sliding her feet as she distanced herself from Devon, whose handsome face turned sour as if seeing her for the first time. Rita stormed off but not before proclaiming emphatically to the crowd that she was indeed *'wife material'* and that Devon missed out on a good thing.

Once the coast was clear the lovebirds embraced each other; the two apologizing profusely between soft kisses. Secrets almost tore them apart and there, in that moment, they vowed that from that day forth, no more new secrets would live between them anymore.

-~-

The sound of the trunk closing jarred Jackie back to reality. A few moments later, Devon entered the kitchen in a bit of a huff.

"Jackie, you still in here?"

"What's taking so long babes time is going?"

His voice bounced off the empty walls echoing in the hallway towards the kitchen. Jackie sat gazing through the window, distant but aware that her husband had entered the room. He was growing impatient because they had a long trip ahead of them.

"Jackie, what's the matter?"

"Sad about leaving?"

Devon's probing questions pierced her already wounded heart. Tears streamed down her round cheeks and onto her bosom before she could even reply. He leaned in and gently wiped away her tears. He cupped her face in his hands and peered deep into her vulnerable soul. Her silence only intensified his guilt, causing him to wonder if he was the reason for her tears. Although they had promised to be honest with each other and their marriage had been flourishing, Devon was now grappling with the weight of their ten-year-old vow.

EMUNAH Y'SRAEL

Island Twist
Book Two
Trevor & Pam

Chapter One

Almost every night around this time she mingled grey goose and cranberry juice; it did the job quickly. The warmth of the spirits rushed into her blood, coursed in her veins, and unlocked her closely held secrets. Each minute that elapsed took with it one more doubt, each second ushered her closer to the path of least resistance. She loved taking the last sip, it was always the sweetest.

It was 11 pm, Pam had just gotten off work late when she decided to make her usual stop at her favorite liquor store. There were many stores between work and home, but The Liquor Palace was perfect for avoiding any run-ins with family or friends. Just a quick in and out, or so she thought, oddly, the store brimmed with customers. *I can't stand being in crowds. Do I really need a drink tonight?* That was a fleeting thought, the knot in her stomach and ever-present crick in her neck reminded her she was going to need some help unwinding.

Great, no parking, Pam banged the steering wheel in frustration. I guess I am going to have to park up the block, parking at a distance was not feasible but often necessary when living in New York.

I can't believe it took me five minutes to find a spot to park. Pam hated walking late at night for many reasons, one being her broad hips and slim waist. Her figure always drew the wrong kind of attention. Since the age of twelve she has been called everything in the book; *sexy body, hot gyal, fluffy, dime piece, chicken head, THOT* you name it, she started taking note of how many men approach her and how many of them use the same ol' tired lines and or insults when they didn't get their way.

What do they want, she lamented, as fate would have it three guys were posted up against the wall in front of the store. Pam slowed down her stride enough to see if she knew them, but she could barely make out their faces. As much as she hated lame pick-up lines, she was not about to let three random dudes stop her from the warm embrace of her beloved habit. Take a deep breath you got this Pam, so she took a deep breath picked her stride back up and walked urgently towards the door.

At the entrance of the store one guy tapped the other motioning him to look in Pam's direction, "um, um um," he hummed.

"Hey, shortie you are looking fly tonight," the slim one said while rubbing his hands against his crotch.

"What's your name ma'?" asked the other as he licked his lips.

She politely smiled, motioning for them to give her passage to enter the store. Her unsuitable suitors refused to move so she pushed past them a bit more aggressively.

"So, you just gonna front like you don't hear me?"

The slim one reached to grab her hand but before he could pull her back the third guy emerged out of the shadows. He had been quietly observing everything and thought the whole scene was about to get out of hand.

"Yo chill!" he barked.

Pam turned around to see who was speaking up on her behalf, it was a tall chocolate man with an unforgettable vibe.

"Sorry about my friends," he said as he rushed in front of her to hold the door open.

She was relieved that she was able to get past the other two, she quickly entered the store, but not before turning back and giving the stranger a smile.

Inside The Liquor Palace the familiar sound of loud banter filled the air. An old man, who was visibly intoxicated, called out lotto numbers to the attendant behind the bulletproof glass.

"I had a dream last night, there I was sleeping in my bed," he said while reenacting the event.

"All of a sudden a large chalk board came down from the sky and there was a voice, yeh there was a voice that sounded like my first-grade teacher Ms. Blackwell." He continued.

"I sure did love her she was one of my fav-o-rite teachers, so anyway the voice said Charlie, Charlie go to the board write these numbers down."

The attendant was rolling his eyes and impatiently waiting for the man to get to the point.

"All I remember was I went up to the board and started writing, 40, 9, 15, 1, 27, 18 and then I jumped up."

"Come on man are you going to place your order or not, we have a lot of customers in here tonight," the attendant said pointing to the line behind him.

"Didn't you hear me Ahmed, I just told you, 40, 9 15, 1, 27,18 these are my lucky numbers," he stammered.

"Now run go tell that."

Charlie slammed his hand on the glass and declared.

"Give me twenty dollars worth of scratch offs too!"

The clerk bent down to tear off a fist full of tickets while he shook his head and shrugged his shoulders.

The Liquor Palace was a chain of stores in New York run by a Pakistani family named the Rhodin's, the night attendant was the owners' first-born son. He was alone and weary of the crowd this time of night, the only thing that made him feel secure was his weapon under the counter and the three-inch bulletproof glass that encased both him and the goods. Business was great for the Rhodin family, but their father always told them not to let it show, "in the hood, you could never be too careful," he would say.

The people from the neighborhood understood the foreigners who ran businesses in their community were just there to exploit them, but what could they do?

Ahmed was visibly disgusted with his drunken customer, murmuring a slur under his breath as he leaned forward to slide the tickets to the old man.

The inebriated man snatched his prized papers and started waving them in the air, dancing and yelling as he walked away,

"I gonna be rich, so rich I'm gonna wipe my behind with dolla, dolla bills ya'll!"

There were about five other men ahead of Pam and with each minute that passed she felt increasingly uncomfortable with the delay. She didn't want to appear bothered so she began busying herself with her phone. After about seven minutes the crowd thinned out, it was finally her turn to order up. She approached the counter calmly, leaned in slightly and spoke in a hushed tone.

"The usual Ahmed," the attendant hesitated before turning to the clear spirit section.

Ahmed had a slight crush on Pam and whenever he saw her his face lit up. He reluctantly retrieved Pam's favorite brand and cautioned her to take it easy. A commotion erupted toward the back. The boozed-up lotto player was visibly angered by his bad luck, he began tearing and throwing his losing lottery tickets in the air like confetti. The floor around him was carpeted with paper. Pam tucked her purchase under her arm securely, like an all-star quarterback; she quickly made her way to the door hoping for a clean escape.

"Lady in the black pants," the voice called.

Pam turned in the direction of the voice; she was halted by his demand. When she turned around, she realized that it was the same old man from the ticket window. He just started talking to her she did not want to laugh but she could not help but notice the floppy red, gold, and green hat atop his head that moved every time he spoke; his salt and pepper locks spilled out on all sides, and he had one shiny gold tooth in his mouth.

Pam froze uncertain of what to do, a smile always worked, she flashed the stranger a closed mouth grin.

"Come here,' he said motioning her over with his wrinkled fingers.

"Me?" Pam mouthed silently looking around for someone else he could possibly be talking to.

"You look just like my baby girl."

"I'm turning sixty-five tonight, and I need to hit this number," He blurted out while raising his hands and patting his chest. Pam nodded her head hoping he would return to his previous activity so she could make her get away. She tried to discreetly wave goodbye, but he motioned for her to wait while he tried his luck again.

"Where are you going, sweetie? Step out the doorway you are going to be my good luck charm, looking just like my baby girl Trina," he repeated several times.

Pam was not Trina but what was she to do, he was making a scene again, so she inched herself over to satisfy his request. When she was close enough to his satisfaction Charlie turned his attention toward his lotto tickets. He proceeded to brace himself up against the wall, penny in one hand ticket in the other.

Pam watched intently as he cocked his head to the side, "come on baby give me what you got!"

Charlie feverishly scratched the gold circles and after blowing the dust from cards the golden particles fell like rain. Pam stood four of these dramatic reveals which were always followed by an "aw man, come on daddy needs a new car."

He continued scratching intermitted stopping to talk to her, "I have nine children and thirty-five grandbabies."

"Wow," she exclaimed.

"Um, huh. That's right and all my babies from the same mama, too!"

"Great," she fiend excitement.

The old man scratched his fifth ticket and this time he didn't grumble or tear it up he just fell on his knees mumbled a few words jumped up and started dancing.

"Pay me, oh yeh Ahmed pay me baby!"

"Forty Acres and a mule baby, here comes my forty acres and a mule."

Charlie abruptly abandoned the conversation without another word, he ran over to the attendant demanding the pay-out he had won.

There was no better time to make her escape, she walked out the door as fast as she could. In her haste she mistakenly bumped into the young man who had held the door open for her earlier. By now his friends had gone off to pursue other females and to her surprise, he had patiently waited for her to exit the store.

"Oh, my bad," I didn't see you she said clumsily.

The collision almost caused her bottle to slip out of her hands. She gripped the vodka by the neck even tighter and took off speedily down the block towards her car.

What a night, all this for a little drink I am really going to have to find a liquor store in another neighborhood. Placing the brown bag gently into the passenger seat, Pam reached over securing it tightly with the seat belt. *The drink is safe now I need some music.* Pam's hands frantically rummaged through the glove compartment for her favorite CD, she murmured something about having to clean her car up tomorrow. *Aha! I got it real love, my jam.* She stretched to put the CD in the player when she heard a faint tap rapped at the window. The tapping startled her; she was still bent over and immediately began looking for something that could double as a weapon. *Yes, empty juice bottle.* A second round of tapping came, this time louder and more rapid. Random thoughts of the worst-case scenario ran through her mind. *It's those dudes from the store, no it's that crazy old man Charlie or maybe…*

Oh, my goodness she thought frantically, *what should I do, drive off, run the person over or wind down my window?*

She contemplated for some time finally deciding to answer the stranger who was bending down to peer through her passenger side window. The glow of the streetlight cast a shadow illuminating only a portion of the person's face. After the third tap, she decided to crack the window just enough to hear the stranger out.

Are my doors locked?

"Excuse me," the stranger pardoned himself politely.

"Yes," Pam answered sternly.

"I am sorry if I may have scared you, but,"

"I had to stop you, and ask are you from around here?"

Is he serious this late at night he is stopping random girls on the street to chat with? When he bent down to speak, she realized it was the guy from earlier, the ebony one. Rolling her eyes in annoyance Pam answered a simple, "No."

"Not much for words I see, it's alright I just have to say I think you are a beautiful woman."

The stranger tried his best to speak like a New Yorker, but she detected an accent. This wasn't the most convenient time to be conversing, but the stranger got Pam's attention because she was attracted to foreign accents. *Oh, I wonder where he is from?* She gave him the once over and reclined in her seat and dropped the empty glass juice bottle that she retrieved earlier. The stranger was still leaning against the car speaking to her through the slit in the window.

"What's your name sweetness?"

"Pam," she scrunched up her face disapprovingly.

"What's your name?"

"Trevor," he replied in a deep voice.

"Well, Trevor, nice to meet you I have to go maybe I'll see you around sometime."

He was cute but Pam had a date with a Grey Goose, and it was rude to keep him waiting. She politely pushed up her window, waved goodbye and drove off. Trevor stood motionless on the sidewalk trying to appear unbothered.

CHAPTER TWO

Pam lived on Jamaica Ave and worked in Rosedale. She lived with her middle-aged mother in a rundown apartment building on the fifth floor, apartment 504 to be exact. Their corner apartment had a balcony that extended from the living room, the one perk Pam enjoyed. She loved chilling out there alone in the summertime; her mother was a nurse who worked the night shift and doubles whenever they were avalible.

Pam pulled up to Greenfield Towers and noticed two neighborhood boys loitering in front of the building. The one with the red shirt and bald head had just finished licking mumbo sauce off his fingers; five chicken wing bones were scattered on the pavement, and he was about toss another.

"Come on Jay you know better than that when you litter you hurt yourself and community." She fussed at him.

Jay's eyes peered down at the brown bag that Pam had tightly grasped in her hands.

"Hurt me?"

"Oh, you mean like that bottle you bring in here dang near every other night?"

His friend cracked up laughing, they both gave each other a dap for his witty comeback.

"That was a good one Jay," he chuckled.

Pam walked off sucking her teeth and pushing her way past the boys, she was not in the mood for their shenanigans. *All I want to do now is go upstairs, take a bath, and chill the night away.* The elevator was out of order again, even though the elevator smelled like a port-a-potty at the county fair, it was better than walking the stairs to the fifth floor. Pam had no choice, she had to do it.

In three minutes flat she arrived on the third-floor huffing and puffing almost ready to pass out. The smell in the stairwell tonight was equal to if not worse than the elevators. Pam gasped as she strained to open the metallic grey door of their two-bedroom apartment. She blindly shuffled through her bag to find her keys, panicking for a minute because it was taking so long to find them; she exhaled a sigh of relief, *here they are finally*!

Pam retrieved the the rhinestone-covered key ring that her boss Janet brought her from Brazil last summer and jiggled the lock. She pushed open the door and darted inside. bolting the door behind her. She neatly put her shoes on the rack, and diligently placed her keys in the bowl on the table counter just like her mother demanded. *Ah*, she sighed as she walked over to the counter and put down her date.

"What a day!" She sighed plopping down on the rose-colored leather sofa.

Her feet were throbbing from standing all day at the salon; come to think of it she wasn't sure when she had eaten last. Pam was a wreck. After a few minutes on the sofa, she did her usual surveillance of the house, she peered into her mother's room to see the bed well made and every item perfectly placed as her mother had left it. Even though her mother had worked nights for the past fifteen years, Pam had a habit of checking her room anyway. She always wished she had parents who would welcome her home in the evening, but that was just a wasted wish, the house was always empty.

It was getting late and even though she had a date she also had work in the morning. *Where is that remote?* She pumped up the stereo on the way to the kitchen. On the kitchen counter, there was a note that read,

> Pam,
> *"I made dinner, hope you had a great day at work. Call me when you get in."*
> -Love Mom

Rice and chicken again, Pam furrowed her brow and slammed the lid of the pot down. *I am not that hungry anyway.* On her way to her room, she spied another note this time a lime green sticky attached to her door,

"Clean this place up, it looks like a pig sty."

Pam's mother's definition of dirty was a few items out of place. *My room isn't dirty, maybe a bit untidy but not dirty. I'll get to that later she thought.* Pam's mother was fussy and difficult. She did not want to hear her mouth on the matter but tonight wasn't a good time to worry about cleaning up.

She turned up the stereo so that she could sing along in the shower. By the time she was ready to relax it was almost one o'clock in the morning. It was a humid summer night and the air conditioning inside was broken. She took some ice from the freezer, took one of her mother's good glasses out of the china cabinet and poured herself a drink. Pam made her way to the balcony with one of the dining room chairs and reclined slowly. Oldies streamed from her favorite radio station, the moon was full, and the night was quiet.

The first sip opened the door to her soul slowly leaking memories of her past down her face. Every time she drank, Pam would rehearse her pain repeatedly blaming her mother, father, Chad, and most of all herself. Twenty minutes had passed, her body was numb and so was her mind. Pam's night gown was soaked from tears, she was all cried out and on the verge of sleep when suddenly; the sound of shattered glass coupled with the warm sensation of dripping blood woke her up. Blood was everywhere on her leg, on the floor and worst of all on her mother's reupholstered dining room chair.

The balcony looked like a crime scene, the liquor glass had witnessed against her, her date had run off and she was left to pick up the pieces. How was she going to explain the broken glass and the bloodstained chair? Worst of all, her mother didn't know she had developed a drinking habit.

Pam stumbled and staggered through the living room on her way to the bathroom, bright red drops of blood trailed behind her, too much to handle in her drunken state. With each step she thought to herself, *I'm too tired I will fix it in the morning*. She managed to drag herself into her room, back up to her bed and freefall into it.

The bed scene is that moment after drinking when you no longer feel anything or care about anything but the opportunity to lie down. That's when you feel it. The ceiling spins, your body is washed away with the euphoric sensation of being weightless, this Pam thought is what made burning through her liver cells all worth it. It lasted a short time and after that, she almost always fell fast asleep.

The slamming of the front door broke the rhythm of her slumber. She immediately knew there was about to be a problem. It was morning time, the alarm was ringing, and Pam was in a haze, she reached over and pressed the snooze for the fifth time but once she heard the door, she knew it was time to get up. Her cleaning job last night was sloppy, stains were everywhere, and her mother was home. Inched here way to the edge of the bed a sharp pain shot through her legs, they were still bloddy and so where her sheets.

"Pam," her mother called.

She could hear her footsteps nearing her room; there was no time to hide so she just lay there.

"Pam, why do you have the house looking like this, it's a bloody mess?"

Pam sat up in her bed.

"Um, sorry mom I was using your glass, and it broke out on the balcony, and a piece cut me here see!" She pandered for her sympathy as she pointed to her bloody leg.

"You know what I am too tired for this, I just worked a double and I don't have the strength for you right now, just make sure you clean this place up before you go to work, you hear me, Pam!"

She dragged herself out of bed to survey the area. She wasn't sure if she had picked up the bottle last night. It was a good thing her mother went to shower, as was her custom when coming home from work. Pam scurried outside to find the bottle and glass shards still lying on the floor. She quickly placed the half-empty bottle into her work bag and proceeded to sweep up the mess she had made. By the time she finished cleaning her mother was in her room dressing and getting ready to sleep.

Pam scurried into the bathroom to shower trying to be extra quiet to avoid any additional confrontation with her mother. The bathroom was like a sauna, Pam's mother loved bathing in scalding hot water. The steam was unbearable; she was still a bit hung-over from last night. She flicked the light on; there was a blanket of moisture across the bathroom mirror. Pam took her index finger and pressed it up against the glass, it squeaked as it glided across the vapor, she doodled for a bit and then wrote in big letters, *why me?*

Every morning was a challenge, this morning she was late. She tapped on her mother's door shouting, "I gotta go, see you later."

"Pam!" Her mother called out, but it was too late. On her drive to the beauty salon, she thought about last night, her throbbing leg, the crazy man at the store and oh yes, Trevor.
I love men with accents she giggled at the thought of Trevor for just a moment but returned to her solemn mood.

She pulled up to work on time; dressed in an oversized t-shirt, worn out jeans, and old hot pink sneakers. Her hair was uncombed, tucked away under favorite Yankee's hat. She was that one girl at the salon whose hair always looked like a hot mess. Her face was beautiful though, almond shaped eyes the color of hazelnuts and flawless smile and a nice body.

Chapter Three

Chad changed Pam forever; things were never the same again after him. He and Pam met in the tenth grade. His family immigrated to Queens from Nigeria, she thought everything about him was intriguing, his real name was Chidi Ebere, but everyone called him Chad. His accent captivated her, his ideas and tales of his homeland awakened the adventure in her. The time they spent together made her long for 'home'.

The two had math, history, and art class together. He was slender; his thick eyebrow framed his handsome face and accented his penetrating stare. Pam thought Chad was smart and assertive, the other children did not feel the same; they made fun of the way he spoke and his style of dress. His parents were traditional and didn't believe in spoiling children, they had no qualms about sending him to school in off brands and no-name sneakers.

Chad's family was very involved in his academic career. His parents, namely his mother, had already declared that he would become a medical doctor in America. Even more bizarre, Chad told Pam that at the age of one his parents arranged his engagement to a girl from his village named Nneka. He assured Pam that he did not share his family's desire to really marry Nneka and that he wanted to eventually pick his own bride. She thought that was weird but that didn't stop the relationship that ensued. The two became almost inseparable; they studied together, wrote poetry together and hung out often. Pam was born in January, and he was born in April of the same year. She often teased him for being his elder and that he should respect her. Their friendship was strictly plotantic, both were young and virgins.

In the spring of sophomore year Chad's mother told him he needed to add some athletics to his curriculum, so he chose running.

"Pam," he said inquisitively while taking a bite of his beef patty. They had stopped at the nearby patty shop to grab a bite after school.

"Yes Chi Chi," she responded wondering what interesting fact he wanted to throw her way now.

"What do you think about me trying out for track and field?"

"I didn't know you ran or even liked running for that matter?"

"Well, I do run, for your info."

"As long as you don't run away from me, I think we should be fine."

The next week Chad tried out for the team; he was selected after three rounds of cuts to join the boys 4 x 100 relay. In addition to his schoolwork, practice began to make demands on his time. He started hanging out more with the guys from the track team during lunch and after school.

Pam noticed the change in him; he became more aggressive, impatient, and secretive about his whereabouts. Chad started speaking differently, trying to hide his accent and walk like the homeboys from around the way. Pam was troubled by this, but she didn't want to lose his friendship, so she never made a big deal about all the changes he was making.

One day Chad and his new homies were at track practice when one boy who always seemed to stir up trouble started poking fun at him. Rodney had a rep with the young ladies and was known for being a *playa*. They had just finished cooling down their muscles after an intense practice; the guys were stretching and putting back on their sweats when Rodney blurted out in front of everyone.

"Chad, I see you and Pam kinda close."

He motioned while flashing a troublesome smirk.

"Did you get some of that yet?" Rodney inquired while using his hands to draw the shape of Pam's behind in the air. Chad was shocked by his forwardness and almost choked on the sports aide he was drinking; the suggestion was embarrassing but he tried to keep his cool.

"Get some?"

His voice cracked spiking in a high-pitched tone. Chad surveyed the faces of all the boys who surrounded him, they eagerly anticipated his answer. He thought long and hard before answering Rodney, the boys hung on to his every word. He wanted to be down with the fellows, but no one warned him Pam was going to be the topic of conversation. He was finally at the threshold of male bonding; he wanted to be cool so badly, the approval of these boys meant a lot. He brooded over his response for what seemed like an eternity, the other boys held their breath waiting for his response. Rodney grew agitated with the silence and repeated the question louder this time.

"Chad did you and Pam get busy or nah?"

Chad stood up from his crouched position on the ground; he stretched his hands over his head and finally broke his silence with a smirk.

"Come on you know how we do, where I come from, we lay it down," he jested in a forced American accent while gyrating his hips.

His answer sent the crowd into an uproar; boys were giving him high-fives and slaps on the back. At first, he smiled and cheered and then as he turned to make his way towards the locker room, a burning sensation swelled in his chest. His smile slowly melted into a frown, he waved to the guys and questioned if he had said the right thing.

Now he had two problems see, there was a bully at school named Charles Broadback and he had a crew of hoodlums who picked on almost everyone. Chad was having some trouble with them, and he needed some guys to have his back. The friends he made at track practice would be perfect if only he was accepted as one of them; he had to tell them what they wanted to hear. He sacrificed his friendship with Pam on the altar of male bravado. Chad little lies returned to haunt him, more than ever he avoided Pam without explanation. A few weeks later she caught up with him demanding to know what was happening between them and why.

-~-

The next day after school they decided to meet at her place, they knew her mom was at work, and they would have the place to themselves.

"Chi Chi, what's wrong?"

Chad paced the floor trying to find way to say what was on his mind. He finally stopped in front of her sitting down at the coffee table.

"Pamela, I like you and I know you like me." *He never calls me Pamela unless it's serious* she pondered.

"Yes, Chi Chi we are friends, I like you as my friend." She was uneasy with the direction of the conversation; Chad's nervous energy filled the room. Pam sat on her mother's rose-colored leather sofa looking straight into his eyes, into his soul and hoping to read his intentions. He got up and started pacing again.

"I can't, I mean I won't, we can't, Pam we are friends right."

"Chad, what's wrong with you?" she urged while pleading with her eyes.

"Why have you been avoiding me, we haven't hung out in weeks, ever since you started running track and hanging with Rodney and them."

She pouted while pointing to his gym bag.

"Pam, things have changed, and we can't keep hanging out, unless."

He paused and at that moment the oxygen in the room seemed to instantly evaporate. Pam gasped for air, it was then she braced herself in anticipation of the or else factor. A million thoughts came crashing in on the banks of her mind, Chad was her only real friend and whatever was on the other side of the or else could possibly take that away.

"The only way we can hang out is if."

"If what," she pressed impatiently growing tired of playing charades.

"Just say what is on your mind Chad," she insisted.

He continued fumbling sounding like a toddler asking for candy before dinner.

"If we well you know," he said, making his way back to where she was sitting.

"No Chad I don't know, just tell me!"

"If we can't well you know," he motioned swiveling his waist in a school boyish manner.

Her eyes enlarged in disbelief, *is he serious*? "Pam, I want to get closer to you," he finally admitted.

"We can't keep hanging out as friends, you and I both know that we want more."

She was dumbfounded, what was he talking about? Their relationship was pure, they were only fifteen and when since was Chad interested in her body. At that moment he slowly pulled her off the rose-colored leather sofa. There they stood in the middle of Pam's mother's living room within inches of each other, heartbeats synching to one rhythm. Chad awkwardly pulled her by the waist, pushing his pelvis up against hers and whispered softly in her ear. "Pam."

Encapsulated in a sea of emotions, she felt a tingling sensation rising from below her navel. She motioned to pull away, but his grip was more powerful than hers. He felt her uneasiness; he took one hand off her waist and used it to caress her face.

"Look at me Pam." he beckoned her.

Pam looked away, gazing out the window in disbelief. This was all happening so fast she couldn't find any words to say.

"Pam, I need more of you," Chad proclaimed, gently turning her face towards his.

She felt the warmth of his body, the sweetness of his breath as he pressed his full lips up against hers. These new sensations swept her away; she was no match for the tidal wave of biochemistry that existed between them at that moment. She melted into his arms, overcome by the undercurrent of love. Pam long desired for someone to say they loved her, someone to show her they cared. That day they did nothing but lay there fully clad, embracing one another in the stillness of the night. The beats of their hearts synchronized into one, unaware of time and space.

Chapter Four

The sound of the ringing telephone cut through the stillness and she sleepily answered the call. Chad was still there they had fallen asleep on the sofa, and he could hear a man's voice on the other end.

"Oh, hey Dad," she said in an unenthused manner.

"Is your mom home?" he asked.

"Nope."

"How are things Pamela, remember I always told you if you need anything to let me know." he prompted.

He was full of formalities; Pam learned that quickly as a young girl. *I am going to take you here or take you there* he would promise, she would wait and wait, and he wouldn't show. Whenever she asked about it, he would come up with every excuse in the book.

"Pam," he called, "you still there?"

"I'm good," just sleepy.

"As always," he replied sarcastically.

"Make sure you lock up."

"Ok, Bye Dad."

Jake's wellness calls were more of a nuisance than anything. Pam's father pretended to care so much when it was clear he didn't. He lived quite comfortably on the hill with his wife and children while she and mom had to live in a urinal for a building. Whenever she asked her mother about the situation between the two, she would just roll her eyes and mumble something about it being complicated.

Pam often wondered what caused the rift between her parents, but it wasn't until Aunt Daisy stepped in that she learned the truth. According to Daisy, Pam's mother, Denise, had an affair with a married man, Jake, who was sixteen years her senior. At the time of their fling, Jake was allegedly going through marital problems with his wife, Nancy. Denise, a college graduate at the age of twenty-two, was ambitious and had a promising future. Despite their age difference and Denise's less-demanding nature, Jake claimed to have, "fallen in love with her."

They had a 'live in' relationship unbeknownst to Denise's parents or Jake's wife Nancy. He moved out of the house and got an apartment with Denise. This was around the time that Pam was conceived. Their relationship only lasted for fifteen and a half months; seven months after Pam was born, he decided that he couldn't do it anymore. In a sudden stroke of conscience, he declared one day, out of the clear blue, that "his wife and three children needed him more."

Just like that, it was over. Denise was on her own at twenty-three years old with a toddler to take care of. It all happened so fast. A few months after he left Denise got evicted from their apartment. Denise and the baby ended up applying for welfare and food stamps; she was devastated and felt isolated from her family.

Aunt Daisy went on to explain that after that they moved from place to place until Denise found the apartment at Greenfield Towers. She worked her way off welfare, finished school and became a nurse. After Jake she lost her free spirit and became a work-a-holic.

Pam gazed at the wall clock; it was getting late. She walked over and tapped Chad on the bottom of his foot. Chad never, I mean never liked to wear socks. No matter how cold it was he would say, *"where I come from, we didn't were socks, I don't like them they suffocate my feet."* His sockless foot wiggled a bit, but he didn't stir much after that.

"You need to get up now!"

He wasn't really sleeping he had heard the entire conversation with Pam and her father and waited for her to return to him in hopes of, well you know them getting closer.

"Chad it's getting late you have to go now; your parents will start looking for you."

His parents required good grades, house chores, a part-time job and a positive attitude; in exchange, they gave him a little bit of freedom. He didn't have many friends, but he did have a lenient 10 o'clock curfew.

"What time is it he asked," feigning sleep.

"9:45 pm"

He jumped up hurriedly gathering his things. Pam stood leaning against the sofa watching as he scrambled to get his things together. Her mind was heavy with what he proposed that day.

"Ok, I'm ready," he announced.

They walked to the door; Chad felt that his best friend was bothered but he didn't have the time to talk. On his way out he turned back, leaned against the doorpost, and gazed affectionately into her eyes. The thoughts of what he had said were pasted on the walls of her mind, things were different now, and she was uncomfortable. Pam closed her eyes to hide the nakedness of her thoughts.

"Think about what I said."

He awkwardly pulled her close and hugged her; every muscle in Pam body was stiff. She simply threw her reply behind him as he ran down the hallway, "ok."

A cocktail of emotions stirred inside confused yet intoxicated by the sensations she now felt for Chad. The lines of their friendship blurred by his "proposition." Pam poured over everything that night. She obsessed over their relationship, how much he meant to her and the tough decision she had to make. In the wee hours of the night, she tossed and turned, waking up before the alarm, before her mother pushed the key in the door.

I am not prepared to lose Chad; he is the only person that makes me feel wanted or even loved. Things were noticeably strained between them for the next few weeks. He occasionally stopped by but did not stay long. Their conversations grew shorter and shorter, neither having anything new to say. Chad had formed a singular thought now and nothing else mattered. There was no one that she felt she could turn to. Pam was an only child for her mother, on matters of the relationship as you can imagine her mother was distant and dismissive. Her aunt Daisy was the only one willing to share intimate details about life with her, but she had her own problems.

Daisy was Denise's baby sister, the proud mother of seven children with three different baby fathers. She often quarreled with the first two men about not supporting and or being there for her children. The last baby's father was currently in jail for shoplifting pampers and formula. She gave him credit for at least trying, so she vowed to wait and be faithful to him. You had to be mindful when visiting Aunt Daisy's, depending on the day you might be drafted in as her star witness for one of her many kangaroo court debates.

Aunt Daisy's cramped three-bedroom apartment was always filled with hungry babies, and women stopping by to buy bootleg purses and perfume. Her life was full of drama, she was Pam's own little hood Soap Opera. After thinking about her options Pam decided that she wasn't up for the 'rah-rah' or for her mother finding out about Chad, so she kept it to herself.

Spring break and Valley High had a two-week recess. Pam had no special plans and neither did Chad. Her mother was rarely home; the friends had the place all to themselves. Pam contemplated if this would be the time that she would agree to Chad's proposition. Over the next few days, like clockwork, he came and went. They ate, watched TV, and listened to music and then nothing. The tension between them grew, words had become taboo there was only one thing Chad wanted to hear. He silently pressured her until her unwilling mind produced the gems she had hidden deep within. He was the miner and she the gold.

She was not ready, but time melted away like the butter on the warmed toast she served him that morning for breakfast. They 'played house' for the past week and now over mint tea, Orange Juice, and wheat toast. Chad was ready to cash in on his investment. He needed this; he envisioned and declared it to be so, all he needed now was for it to happen.

"Pam," he whispered her name softly while breaking off a piece of toast.

"Yes Chi Chi," she answered hesitantly.

"Are you ready now?"

Pam had just raised the glass of O J to take a sip, his words felt like the first drop of summer rain, flooding her heart, and breaking her will. Pam knew she wasn't a 'fast, loose, slack' girl, she never wanted to be that girl, but there was no one around to secure the borders of her virginity. Chad the friendly intruder had breached her gates and was about to enter her house making away with the best part of her. *He is different, we are friends, and he won't hurt me,* she reasoned.

All morning they silently waltzed around the topic, the tension was mounting, pressure building and then, finally she broke. She disappeared to her room and returned in a nightgown. Behind her back was a pillow. Chad's back was turned facing the TV, she crept up behind him yelling, "pillow fight."

She playfully hit him; he sprung from the sofa and began to wrestle with her. He guessed this was her way of breaking the ice. He chased her around the living room, Pam jumped over chair dodged his advances, giggled, and taunted him. This play riled him up, Chad playfully threw her down on the sofa. All resistance fled at that moment, he eased his way on top of her and they kissed for the very first time.

"Pam," his eyes begged the question.

"Yes Chi Chi?" she answered reluctantly.

For weeks he had asked, pressured, and cajoled but for some strange reason, he wasn't prepared for her to say yes. None the less he proceeded. They awkwardly engaged one another, she was in pain, she cried, and he wiped her tears. She bled, they both were afraid, he thought he had wounded her, he did. She cleaned herself up, he packed up his belongings and went home with her prize.

CHAPTER FIVE

Pam frantically searched the halls of the school; she and Chad were drifting apart he was spending most his time afterschool at track practice. Normally she didn't bother him, but this was urgent. Six weeks passed since the time they lay together, six weeks passed since her flow ceased. She was not prepared for this, nor did she know what to do. She heard about high school girls getting pregnant and having to drop out of school, but she never thought it would be her. He was by the track talking smack in a crowd of boys, she waved him over to her.

"Ah, man Chad there goes Pam," Rodney said.

She sure is fine," another added.

"Fine you mean a dime, I would like to get a chance with her," Rodney replied.

Chad couldn't believe that they were speaking about Pam like this. He wanted to fight right there, but he reasoned to just let it go. Instead, he jokingly said, "Come on man chill out, she is mine."

He made his way toward Pam ushering her out of the eyesight of his girl crazed friends.

"What's good Pam," he smiled irresistibly.

She fiddled with her hair; bit her lip, nervously drawing lines in the gravel with her foot.

"Chad, I have," she paused a long nerve-wracking pause.

"Never mind," she whined as and turned to walk away.

Chad pursued her, "Pam please wait. What is it?"

By now tears welled up in her eyes, *what if he rejects me, what if I end up like Aunt Daisy?*

"Come on Pam, just tell me you can tell me anything."

Amid a long exhale the words tumbled out of her mouth, "Chad I haven't seen my period."

"What is that suppose to mean?"

His eyes glossed over with disbelief.

"I might be pregnant Chad."

Her head fell as she spoke those words.

Chad stood frozen in time; the only thing that moved was his thoughts. *The crew never warned me, this was my first time, how was I supposed to know, my parents, Nnkea, what have I done?*

"Are you sure?" Those three words were all he could finally muster up.

He didn't move to hug her, she stood inches in front of him, crying and waiting for him to embrace as he did that day but instead all he could say was, "I will meet you at your house after school."

Pam reluctantly agreed.

After practice, he arrived at her mother's house. He knocked on the door with his usual code, two knocks wait and then a succession of one knock until she answered. When the door opened, Chad was surprised to see Pam's face and eyes all swollen from crying for hours. He entered with a curious brown bag tucked under his arm.

"Here," he handed it to her, take this.

"What is it?"

"Just open it," he demanded.

Opening gifts were often reserved for joyous occasions; the possible pregnancy at fifteen was not a gift or a joyous time. Inside the bag was an at-home-pregnancy test.

"Take it," he urged.

"According to the box, it can tell if you really are pregnant all you have to do is pee on the stick."

"Come on Pam we have to know for sure before we get all worked up."

She reluctantly took the box and opened it; she sat lifelessly as she attempted to read the instructions. Chad made his way to the kitchen to get her some water.

"Here drink this."

She took the glass but could not take but a sip, "Drink the whole thing, come on Pam stop playing!"

Playing? Was this a game?

Let's go to the bathroom, he bossed her around trying to take control of the situation. He stood anxiously outside of the bathroom door waiting to hear her flush the toilet. After moments of quiet, he barged in unannounced. Pam was squatting over the toilet clumsily trying to hold still and pee on the tiny stick.

"Chi Chi what are you doing?"

"I can't wait, I have to see this for myself come on Pam, pee!"

"I can't pee with you standing there," she waved him out of the bathroom.

"Ok then," he jested, "I will turn my back."

"Chi Chi," she whined, "will you stop playing, this is serious."

"I am serious now let me hear you pee and don't miss the stick."

This was the Chi Chi she had grown to love as a friend, but now was not the time for jokes. She attempted to laugh at his insistence on her peeing in his presence, but instead, she settled on a crooked smile.

That moment was short lived followed by a gut-wrenching scream.

"Noooo, this can't be," Pam bellowed.

"No, this can't be!"

"What are we going to do?"

Startled by her response he grabbed the stick from her hand while she was still sitting half-clad on the toilet. There it was, big and bold, two lines, the box says two lines means proof positive of pregnancy. Chad envisioned his parents; he wondered if he would get beat or shipped off back home. She imagined the voice of her mother browbeating and disapproving of her. Pam's eyes welled up again, this time the tears streamed with what seemed like an endless flow of worries.

"You did this to me," she screamed.

"You wanted to get closer, well is this close enough for you now?

He had never seen her like this before.

"You wanted to do it; I didn't make you do anything!"

What! Are you serious? She screamed.

Pam grew angry; she wiped her tears and looked him square in the eyes, ending up like her mother was not an option. She commanded to know, what are we going to do?

She pressed him for answers, but it was futile, he was a schoolboy and she a simple schoolgirl. They were not prepared for sex or parenthood after all they were children themselves. What are we going to do; she kept repeating the same ol' question until he gave a satisfactory answer.

"We?" he replied.

"Yes, Chad we, like as in you and I, Us!"

"Look Chad, we are only fifteen but together we can make this work."

"How about we get married?"

"Married," Chad scoffed.

Things had gone too far if it wasn't for me listening to those silly schoolboys, I wouldn't be in this situation right now. My parents are going to box me up and ship me off back to Nigeria, he fretted.

"Pam, come on why are you acting like you don't already know, I am engaged to Nneka back home. Our families had agreed to this since we were one-year-olds. I am here to finish school and become a doctor. I can't do this right now."

She squinted her eyes and cocked her head to the side, "Why you coming at me sideways Chad"?

"What do you mean by 'this'"?

"My parents will not be pleased and what about yours what are you going to tell them?"

She waited all of two seconds and then blurted out, "the truth."

"We are going to tell them, the truth."

"But Pam we are just friends," he sid sounding rather childish.

"But Chad friends don't have sex," she mocked.

"I know, he finally confessed that was my stupid idea, the boys at school pushed me to do it."

Pam could give two rats behind about who made him do what. All she cared about was what was going to happen next. At the end of hours of deliberation, they both decided that they would have to tell their parents the truth. Chad went first. His mother blew her top. She spouted disdainful words at him and his little "fast, no good American girlfriend." Pam got the brunt of it. Chad's mother called her a "bad breed", girl who the devil sent to rob their family sucess. Chad never came to Pam's aid.

"You want to embarrass us son."

"You," she shouted pointing her finger in his chest.

"You know that we engaged you to Nneka," she sung her name sweetly smiling while recanting the story but instead you chose to "em-ba-rass us with that dirty girl Pam!"

We sent you to school to learn not to lay around with the girls there. His mother grew weary of scolding him, so she turned to his father who was seated at the table eating jollof rice and stew chicken.

"Say something Deke', your son is going to bring down trouble on me, ohh!"

His mother was doing such a good job of scolding Chad that his father was at a loss for words. What else was there to say? "No worry my wife I will speak to him alone when you are finished," Deke replied to her in-between bites.

She turned her face back toward her son in disgust, "move from me before I," His mother motioned to hit him with the broomstick she waved through the air, Chad ducked and jumped off the chair and ran to his room.

"I have a mind to send that BOY back home," she shouted loud enough for him to hear. Calm down my wife, we will work this out.

"Work it out, he will ruin us, my husband, shame us in the street. Do you want it to be said that Deke's and Rosa's son is a de-ge-na-rate?"

"No worry I will deal with them," mothered promised, referring to Pam and Chad. Beating her chest and waving her hands in victory she continued, "I will have my doctor and my traditional wedding if it takes my last breath."

Pam's mother and father could hardly speak amicably about anything. Her mother was still resentful of him leaving her to raise Pam all alone. When Pam told them both she received nothing but silence. For three days Pam tip-toed around her mother, her silence on the matter was deafening. On the third morning, her mother came into her room after working a double and asked one question, "Who is he?"

Denise coordinated a visit for herself and Pam to meet Chad's parents at their home. He had been forbidden by his parents to see or visit Denise since that fateful day. His free time had been revoked, and he was confined to home and school. Denise had asked Jake to come along, but as usual, something had come up.

The reception at Chad's house was cold. Rosa, his mother, was like a tigress poised to strike her prey. Chad's father was relaxed and unassuming, watching as the conversation unfolded.

"Have a seat, Ms.-" Rosa motioned towards Denise as to ask her name.

"Jones, Denise Jones," she responded.

"Well Ms. Jones, so you are 'this things' mother?"

Denise furrowed her brow, "Excuse me who are you calling a thing?"

Rosa didn't stop to clarify, "and her father, does she even have one?"

"If she didn't how could she have been born."

"Oh, so you have a mouth," Rosa said amused.

"Well good we can drop the formalities, Ms. Denise."

"This is my home, here is my husband, this is my son, who will become a reputable and successful doctor," Rosa asserted snobbishly.

Rosa dominated the conversation; her husband interjected politely, "Rosa my wife let our guest speak." She glared over at him, kissed her teeth then turned her attention back to Denise and Pam, "Ok, speak!" she commanded.

"Well as my daughter had told me your son, encouraged her to lay with him. She was a virgin and he impregnated her."

"What!" Rosa leaps from her seat, "that is a dirty lie, your daughter seduced my son with her nasty ways." Her hands were now on her hips and her chest puffed with pretentiousness. As I told you my son had no reason to do such a thing, he is going to be a doctor and your daughter will probably end up at some low-class job or on welfare or something."

"ROSA!" Deke shouted, "stop being so disrespectful."

She fanned off her husband's rebuke and continued.

"It's, true Deke' look at them, she is not fit to tie Chidi's shoes much less."

Pam sat numbed; she was physically present but could no longer feel anything as Chad's mother berated her and her mother. She rubbed her belly mulling over the type of future her unborn child would have. Chad sat still; he dared not mumble a word because he was no match for his mother. Pam and Chad tried earnestly not to stare at one another; any notion of eye contact or emotional connection might get them both double slapped.

"So, Ms. Denise, where do you work, if even you work at all?"

Denise looked at Rosa wondering how a woman so vile was able to keep a man when she was all alone. She folded her arms and steered at Rosa, "aren't we hear to talk about Chad and Pam?"

"Yes, you got that right," Rosa snapped back.

"What do you propose they do Rosa since you seem to have all the answers," Denise challenged.

"Finally, you have come to your senses," Rosa rose from her seat suddenly clapping her hands together frightening everyone in the room.

"My Chidi is already engaged to a girl named Nneka in my village back home. He can't and will not marry your daughter under any circumstances. I don't know about your culture, but we are not interested in any illegitimate grandchildren."

"Rosa, stop it," Deke' commanded.

"Come on my husband, let me tell her."

Where we come from things are done correctly. If you were watching your daughter, she wouldn't have seduced my son with her American ways."

American ways? Seduce? Pam began to wonder, what exactly did Chad tell his parents.

"We suggest and I even more strongly suggest that you do as I have heard many of your kind do."

Denise grimaced; she was even more confused by Chad's parents than she was about the pregnancy situation. *My kind, this woman is about as dark as I am, is she crazy or something?*

When Deke' heard enough he made his way to the front of the living room floor and cleared his throat.

"Denise is there some way we can get in touch with Pam's father?"

"Yes, he is around but I will have to see." she said despondently.

Rosa huffed, crossing her big thighs at the center. She busied herself with the embroidery on her kaftans so as not to disrespect her husband as he spoke. *I don't know what he is doing, no need to meet anyone else, I don't like her, and she and her supposed pregnancy can go.* Deke's words fell on deaf ears; Rosa was too busy glaring at Pam, if she could at this moment, she would give her something to make her unpregnant. Her wide eyes narrowed, *yes that's it, I will make sure she gets un-pregnant. My son will be a doctor!*

By the time the meeting was over the parents agreed to come up with a solution to remedy the indiscretions of their children. That night Rosa nagged her husband continuously, she threatened if things didn't go her way, she would ship their only son off back to Nigeria.

Over at Pam's her mother remained relatively quiet. Denise grappled with putting her pride aside to consult with Jake on the matter; she was not willing to have Pam end up like her. She did not want to raise another baby alone with no father at home. Jake did what he usually did, offered empty words and vein jestures; she grew frustrated and hung up on him. Denise was convinced that she had to make Pam do the unthinkable.

Pam's mother called Rosa on her break from work, she hated to agree with her but in her narrow thinking, there was no other choice. They both refused to raise the child of their teenage children. Chad's mother told him if he didn't persuade Pam to do *it* that he would be on the next thing smoking. Everyone seemed to have decided for her. No one asked her what she thought, what she wanted or what she was willing to do. Even her mother hinted at the idea of her being on her own if she did not comply with the plan.

CHAPTER SIX

Everyone except Pam agreed that this was the best option. The stench of that day will be forever etched in her mind. Rosa, Chad, and Pam's mother accompanied or more like ushered her to the clinic. Rosa told Chad that she wanted to be there to make sure the "dirty gal Pam," gets it done. Rosa had no sensitivity for the process, when they arrived inside, she took the lead. She demanded paperwork, ordered the procedure, and even requested to have a sidebar with the doctor.

"Are you the girl's mother?" The receptionist inquired.

"No see her irresponsible mother over there, I am his mother," she said pointing to Chad.

"Ma'am if you are not the girl's mother then please take a seat, we have to protect the patient's privacy," the red-headed receptionist turned back toward her computer screen.

"Privacy, my foot," Rosa scoffed.

Rosa begrudgingly took a seat in the front row; she placed her oversized Ankara bag in the empty chair beside her. Her eyes panned the room giving a look of disapproval to all the "careless gals," who had gone off and gotten themselves pregnant.

Ms. Jacobson a voice behind a blue masked called, "Pam Jacobson." She stood up reluctantly, hesitantly looking back at her mother's face for any indication of saving her from this moment. There was none to rescue her, Denise's eyes were vacant. She looked over at Chad who had his head down the entire time pretending to be occupied fixing his sandals. Rosa quickly grew impatient with Pam's; she fanned her off to the attending nurse but not before barking, "Just go already!"

A heavyset blonde nurse named Casey took her vitals she gave her a white robe, instructing her, "take your clothes off and put on this," it was a cloth white robe patterned with dog bones. Pam fantasized about childhood, she wished she could sprinkle fairy dust and disappear, but this was real, and she was alone.

Her body was covered with goosebumps and her hands shivered from the cold temperature in the office. Now that she had taken off her jeans and T-shirt, she realized that her body was changing. Her belly had gotten a little rounder, and her breasts were fulling out. She turned around in the mirror that hung on the back of the door and continued to rub her stomach terrified of her baby's fate.

Pam's parents never taught her much about God; the only prayer she knew by heart was her bedtime prayers, at that moment she had the urge to pray. Her heart overflowed with grief, she opened her mouth, but no words came out, just tears unstoppable stream of tears came flowing from her eyes falling and crashing against the cold sterile floor. A stocky middle aged European doctor entered the room, Pam was still on her knees, and he was unfazed.

"Get up I have a full schedule today," he motioned for her to sit on the table she inched her way up he manhandled her legs into the stirrups. "Try and relax, this will be quick."

A strange sound ensued followed but excruciating pain. After what seemed like an eternity the procedure was over, Pam was given discharge papers and sent home. That day a piece of Pam's soul died; they buried it in a trash bag and deposited it in a dump. Her mother never spoke of it again.

-~-

The next two years of high school were a blurr, Pam and Chad parted ways; she could not bring herself to even look at him after what he put her through. She buildt a wall around the memory of that day, but pieces of it kept spilling into her now.

Pam's father, Jake, bought her a secondhand car for her graduation. Unsure whether it was out of guilt or pride, she accepted the keys to her four-year-old, candy apple red Honda Civic. The car boasted a sunroof, luxurious leather seats, and a thumping sound system. Admittedly, the vehicle boosted Pam's self-esteem. To prepare for getting her license, Jake provided Pam with a state-issued driver's manual to study.

The phone rang, sleepily Pam answered, "Hello."

"Hey, baby girl it's your dad."

"Get yourself ready, I'm coming to get you."

"Get me, really? Are you serious this time or,"

"Trust me, Pam, I know I have disappointed you in the past, but I am two minutes from your house so get your clothes on we are going for a ride."

Pam hurried, brushed her teeth, washed her face, and combed her hair into a ponytail. Before stepping out she doubled back and decided to throw on her favorite New York Yankees baseball cap for good measure. Outside right in front of the building was her father in her new car, he let down the window as she exited the building.

"Come on baby girl lets go."

This is the most alive Pam has felt in a long time, she finally had her dad all to herself even if it was for a few hours. They drove over to the big baseball stadium parking lot.

"Now Pam, I want you to remember all you learned."

"It's time to show me what you got!"

She smiled, Pam longed for these moments, it took eighteen years for at least one of her parents to really care about her. She wanted to talk about more than driving, but she decided to be present,

He watched and instructed as she drove around and around the parking lot. Pam slowly reversed, made her three-point turns and practiced parallel parking. An hour had passed; Jake was satisfied with Pam's driving.

"Let's grab something to eat," he suggested.

"Ok."

Pam could not believe she was out and about with her dad like this. His new freedom of time made her wonder where his wife and children were. She wanted badly to ask him about them but decided against it. *I don't want to ruin the moment, today is our day.*

At breakfast, she felt like a child all over again. She found herself studying her father's face, his eyes, the shape of his ears, the way he stuttered when trying to say words that started with t's; being with him helped her momentarily forget about her loss.

"Are you ready Pamela?" he asked.

"I have to get going now," slowly standing up searching his pockets for the keys. Pam was hesitant to speak, tortured by the possibility of being visible, her veiled smile was no longer enough to cover her pain. She wanted to hold her father accountable for leaving her, she wanted to hug him like she was five and he was her superhero. How could she say anything without releasing a torrent of fermenting emotions, aged and barreled under years of abandonment?

By the time they got back into the car her thoughts were palpable, he pretended not to feel them clawing at him. He quickly let the window down, "What a beautiful day."

Pam just stared at him, so many thoughts hopped and skipped through her mind. *Ask him about mom, why did me, does he love me?* By the time Pam worked up enough nerve to speak Jake had driven her back to the apartment.

"Great!" he declared as if he had just accomplished something monumental.

"We're here," he continued.

"You are road ready my dear," he smiled broadly.

Pam faked a smile; she thanked him for the car, the breakfast, and his time.

Chapter Seven

Pam's life was mediocre at best. At the ripe age of nineteen, she had slipped into a mild depression. Her days were filled with junk food, sleeping, and watching ratchet reality T.V. shows. Somehow watching drama unfold in other people's' lives gave her a twisted sense of satisfaction. College was out of the question her mother says she couldn't afford it.

"Pam, you need to find a job or else," her mother said one night before leaving for work. No one else knew about the unplanned pregnancy or the abortion that Pam was forced to have. Aunt Daisy did notice a change in Pam, but she could not put her finger on what it was, Daisy's life was so wild she never had enough time to find out.

That summer Pam found a job as a hair washer at a beauty salon named Fly Girls in Rosedale. Her new car was one of the reasons she got the job, reliable transport. The other salon girls admired her whip, sometimes they would ask for rides home, Pam always said yes. She looked up to them because they seemed confident in control of their lives.

The owner of the shop's name was Janet, she took a liking to Pam from the first day; she got the job on the spot. Janet was gregarious, with a lot of love to give. She loved eating and cooking. Janet always brought her latest dish to work for the ladies; there was always so much food around the women joked about why Janet opened a beauty salon as opposed to a restaurant. The job was menial, but it was a start Pam was just glad for the opportunity to get out of the house and meet new people. The salon girls treated her like a sister, they loved her head full of kinky curls.

"Oh, Pam you so pretty girl, when you gonna let me do your hair?" Keke playfully teased her.

Keke was a new stylist; she was a few years older than Pam. She recently finished cosmetology school and was trying to build her clientel. Keke spent her days at the shop thumbing through urban hair magazines studying the latest hairstyles.

"Not today, Keke, maybe later," she responded trying to be polite. Pam wasn't in the mood for getting her hair done or dressing up for that matter. The last thing she wanted to more attention. The salon's busiest days were Friday and Saturday, sometimes Pam didn't stop washing heads till nine o'clock at night. After a couple of months on the job she would learn to stay late just in case, there was usually one woman desperate to get her head done who always arrived ten minutes before closing.

"Janet please let me in," they would plead.

They would have some sob story about a wedding, graduation, or an anniversary that they needed to "look good" for. Sometimes Janet was so tired and ready to go she would ask them to please come back in the morning. That's when they started begging.

"A wash and style shouldn't take long," they would plead from outside the locked door doing prayer signs and dancing. This was usually the moment that Janet gave in; she didn't have the heart to turn them away like that so she would count on Pam to wash their heads and get them started in the chair.

Pam became Ms. Reliable, Janet counted on her to arrive early and leave late. One Thursday morning she arrived at work to find many clients already waiting. They were all talking about that weekend, the atmosphere buzzed with anticipation. Pam had apparently forgotten about the three-day weekend coming up, the women all showed up early in hopes that they would get a jump start on getting their hair done. They vibrantly chatted about who was going to be there, which man was sweating them, whose husband was sleeping around and who had the sexiest outfit for later.

Pam sat beside the receptionist half watching the ladies with her other eye glued on the TV. Her job was to wash and prep, all the chairs were full, so she waited patiently to be able to take the next one. About two o'clock that afternoon the chime from the door went off yet again. This time the jingle didn't cease after a few seconds, the sound trailed behind the woman who had just come in. Pam gave her the once over to see where the chink-chank sound was coming from. It was the bangles; the woman's bangles reached the mid arm, and she sparkled like a disco ball. Everyone in the salon stopped too, this client commanded their attention, she was loud, animated and spoke with a thick accent.

"How can I help you?" the receptionist greeted her.

"Bwoy, it packs in here!"

"Yes, we have been busy all day."

"Again, how can I help you?"

"Oh, me?" the woman asked pointing to herself.

"Yes, you what can we do for you today."

"Bwoy, me nuh inna no long wait," she complained.

"Ma'am is there something we can do for you," the receptionist was clearly bothered now because the customer was making her miss the good part of her show.

"Lady don't get so uptight relax nuh."

She immediately began to elaborately describe the type of hairstyle she wanted. She raised her hand making gestures up to the nap of her neck and slanting down her face.

"Me want an updo wid a swoop bang," she said proudly.

"Excuse me," the receptionist interrupted unsure if she understood her request.

The customer let out a big sigh as if clarifying would cost her, she rolled her eyes and started over.

"Ok, lady me want you to wash and blow dry my hair, den," she bent down to pick up the bag she had placed on the floor during her earlier demonstration. The woman fished around for a second and retrieved a plastic bag with a kinky bright red weave. She clapped her mouth loudly before continuing, "then me want yuh fe put dis red weave inna me up do, you know fe give it some puff appeal."

Humoring herself she let out a hearty laugh, "hey...hey me a go look good this week."

"Oh, you mean you want a ponytail with the weave you brought?" she asked.

Pam sat watching the back and forth between the two of them as if it was a grand slam tennis match. The customer was so unlike anyone she had seen come in before she couldn't help but giggle a bit.

"Weh you a laugh fa," the customer said pointing towards Pam direction.

Pam never answered, she just smiled. The woman turned her attention back to the receptionist, "How long me haffi go wait now ma'am," her voice raised in anticipation for the answer.

"Well as you can see, we have several clients ahead of you, you are more than welcome to wait, and someone will be with you as soon as possible.

"Wait," she blurted out.

"Ma'am I am a busy woman me can't sit down all day."

Just then she turned to look at Pam, while still talking to the receptionist she asked, "well wah bout she."

"She who ma'am," she asked confused.

"She", the customer pointed straight at Pam.

"I see her sitting there, does she work here?"

"Yes, she works here, but she is the wash girl," answered the receptionist.

"Well, a nuh wash me want, me want she fe do me hair," the customer was clearly set on her request.

The client pushed her way past the receptionist, took Pam by the hand and went over to the washing station. Once there she bent down placing her knock-off designer Guess duffle bag full of hair beside her. She put her purse in her lap and sat in the chair. Pam paused for a moment; she was unsure about this and wanted to check with Janet to see if doing her hair was alright. Janet saw the whole ordeal and assured Pam it was alright after all the shop was full and she didn't want the woman to make any more of a scene.

Over at the wash sink, the woman impatiently waited for Pam's return. As soon as Pam returned, she rudely demanded to know, "Ah weh you did go, bathroom? Mek sure you wash yuh hand before yuh touch me head."

"No, I didn't go to the bathroom but yes I will wash my hands."

"So, what's your name?" she spoke slowly and purposely to make sure Pam understood her.

"Well, my name is Pam."

"What' yours?" she asked politely.

"Who me, my name is Rita, and I am from," she stopped midway and then playfully continued, "Guess."

Pam thought for a minute she heard the accent but was uncertain which island she didn't want to run the risk of blurting out the wrong thing. Rita looked like the type of woman who would embarrass her.

"I am Jamaican," she laughed, "can't you tell."

Pam smiled as she unfolded the beauty smock, lined Rita's neck with a paper tissue and fastened it.

"Ah, dat too tight, you a try choke me?"

"No, I'm so sorry," Pam replied nervously as she quickly readjusted the smock.

Rita leaned back into the chair and began to hum as she waited for her wash. Pam was a fast learner, and all the women loved the way she washed their hair. Rita was no exception after the wash was down, she could not help but boast about that being the best hair wash she ever got inna America.

Pam nodded her head in approval, smiling while she shyly responded, "thank you." Now the fun and games were about to begin, Pam had watched women getting their hair done hundreds of times since she has been here but to be doing it herself, now that was a different story. She borrowed the spare hairdryer from the back and took Rita to the side booth that was used for storage.

"No stress, I see you nervous I know you can do it; you work in a beauty salon for crying out loud."

Pam needed that vote of confidence. She proceeded to blow dry and oil Rita's hair and roots. Soon after the noise of the blow dryer subsided Rita turned her attention to Pam.

"You want a piece of gum," she asked as she shoveled a stick into her mouth.

"No thank you," Pam reluctantly answered searching for the tools to do the ponytail.

She looked her up and down while she popped her chewing gum loudly. Rita leaned forward in the chair, tapping her neon green acrylic nails against the chair handle. Pam tried to ignore the sound as she was stressed looking for an extra tail comb, gel, and flat iron. *I hope I get this right; I don't want her to embarrass me, but I could use the extra money from this.*

"You are a pretty girl," before Pam could turn around to respond Rita continued.

"But me a try figure out why you dress so, you look frumpy and well like one ol' woman.'" Judging by her early interaction Pam decided against taking Rita's critiques too personally, it was apparent that she was just an outspoken person.

"You need fe cute up yuhself." She suggests while readjusting her clothes.

"Ok, I'm finally ready," Pam said relieved.
She had found a jar of unopened black gel, a packet of rubber bands, hair pins, and a tail comb. She went to work on Rita's head sculpting and re-sculpting her ponytail just right. She added in the weave securing it with hairpins and thread. After about an hour of tugging and pasting, she was satisfied enough to show Rita what she had done.

Pam took the mirror that hung on the wall and handed it reluctantly to Rita.

"I hope seh you do a good job."

Me too, Pam held her breath as she awaited the reaction.

With a squealing revelation Rita jumped out the chair, "Me love it, she began to model in front of the bigger mirror saying, "a so me cute," she sang while swinging her hips from side to side.

Rita immediately turned her attention back to Pam pointing to her and claiming her spot, "Pam, are my new personal stylist."

Shocked and pleased at her response Pam could not help to correct her, "but Rita I am not a stylist I am a washer girl."

"If me seh you a stylist, then you a stylist."

"Stop acting so prim and proper," she teased.

"How much do I owe you?" she asked as she dug for a change purse.

Pam was so excited that she forgot to ask Janet for pricing. Upon her return, she found Rita on the phone talking to someone trying to explain how cute she looked in her new hairdo.

"I will send a pic so you can see it, yeh me will call yuh later."

She hung up the phone and immediately began to pose, taking countless selfies to try and find which one suited her best. Pam cleared her throat to get her attention.

"So how much me owe you, Pam?"

"Forty-Five dollars," Rita echoes Pam, by now she had stopped taking the pictures and put the phone on the counter.

"Forty-five dollars, a so you price dem high."

"Well, it's alright, I will pay cause mi look good and neva haffi wait. She counted out two twenties and a five and handed it to Pam. Then she said, "Have a seat Pam," Rita presumptuously instructed her.

"I like you, you a go be my stylist, but you have fe do me a favor you haffi go pep up yourself cause anybody who a work fe Rita haffi ready."

"Ok."

She rose from her seat and gathered her belongings; Pam volunteered to show her out. Rita strutted through the main area like she was a reality TV star or something. All the women ogled her 'up do' it was different yet simple. She waved bye and told Rita to remember what she said.

CHAPTER EIGHT

That day Pam washed twenty heads; at the end of the night, she had earned $145 including the monies she earned from Rita. Her mother didn't require her to pay bills yet, but she was responsible for paying for her own car insurance. Shopping and going out wasn't her thing so most of the money Pam made was saved for a rainy day.

One night after work Keke from the salon invited her to a party. Pam's instinct was to say no but remembering what Rita had said some weeks earlier she decided to loosen up a bit.

"Girl where are going?" Pam asked Keke anxiously.

"A house party out on Long Island, my crush invited me, girl there are going be some cute guys there."

Keke was snapping her fingers while shaking her neck.

Pam drove as Keke finished her make-up in the mirror, it was dark and hard to see the street signs.

"What did you say the street was again," Pam was trying to get Keke's attention, but she was busy on the phone with some guy.

"Hey what street is it again," she asked the person on the other end of the line.

Keke started waving frantically,

"Turn here, right here Pam on Broadway. They finally made it, there were people outside the house hanging out and drinking. Pam and Keke smelled weed smoke as they entered the house. She was hestitant but Keke was excited, "Gurl there are some fine dudes in here tonight!"

"I am about to go look for my crush, I will be back."

Keke darted away and disappeared into the crowd. Pam wasn't really into meeting new boys, she did see something she was interested in trying out, the bar. She walked over and leaned against the stool waiting for the bartender to come her way.

"What can I get for you," he asked while he shined the glass in his hand.

"I don't know," she finally responded.

"What do you suggest?"

"Well, it depends, but for a pretty young girl like you I would say you need a ladylike drink maybe a Long Island Iced Tea or an Amaretto Sour."

He sounds like he really knows what he is talking about, maybe I should try the long island that sounds New Yorkish. Pam took her drink and made her way to the corner of the room. Just as she was about to take her first sip of the Long Island Iced Tea Keke appeared emerged from the crowd.

"Girl you alright?" she asked, attempting to scream over the blaring music.

Pam nodded, as she took her first sip.

That first taste was everything, and from that moment she was hooked. She felt relaxed and comfortable enough to release her inhibitions. Who knew that someone could mix an elixir that could make your troubles disappear? The discomfort that usually resided in her chest melted away, drops of tingling sensations overflowed in a pool of sweet waters, Pam suddenly felt alive again.

"I'm glad you got a drink, cause girl you need to loosen up," Keke danced her way out of the corner and disappeared again into the crowd.

Pam drank the cocktails with ease, and by her fourth drink, she was ready to party. Pam danced with several men, including Tyrone, Keke's crush. When Keke saw Pam dancing with him, she was ready to call it quits. She walked over in a huff. Keke pulled her sternly by the arm off the dance floor, but Pam was reluctant to go.

"Girl, you are tripping," Keke said in a low voice.

"I've never seen you like this, what has gotten into you?"

Pam was on cloud eight about to jump on nine, she was distracted by her new feeling, she watched as Keke's lips moved but she didn't understand anything she was saying. The entire time Tyrone was still eyeing Pam from the dance floor, after a few minutes of waiting he called her over with his pointer finger.

She blushed and hinted for him to wait.

"Keke, do you think he is cute?"

"Who, no Pam we have to go I am not doing this anymore."

"Keke look, he is calling me," she chirped as she spun her friend around.

Oh, no she didn't, Pam is tripping I am not about to stand here and watch her feel up on my crush. Keke quickly changed the subject, "Girl bye you are drunk, you better come on or I'm leaving you. Remember we have work tomorrow."

She added in work because it seemed as though Pam forgot they were employed at the same place. Keke could easily gossip about her to the rest of the women, after all, they weren't friend-friends more like co-worker-friends.

Drunk, that was a new concept to Pam, she had never gotten drunk in all her nineteen years on earth. She had seen her Aunt Daisy's men get drunk, she had watched movies with women getting tipsy but for her, this was a first. It felt different. She wasn't sure but, in her mind, it felt great.

"Drunk you say Keke, I'm not drunk I feel good," she clumsily uttered waving her finger slowly in the process.

"Are you coming or not?"

Pam nodded at Keke as she walked off, "Give me a sec she shouted while walking back to the dance floor, just one sec."

I can't leave yet this cutie is checking for me, she thought to herself.

By the time Pam found her way back to Tyrone the DJ changed the song. The temperature in the room seemed to rise ten degrees, Tyrone pulled her into his chest, she embraced him flirtatiously placing her hands around his neck. He smiled mischievously and began slowly dancing and humming the melody to the song.

Keke fumed from the corner she had seen enough. Can you believe Pam, *I brought this girl out here, she always moping around the shop and dressing like someone's Granny... and now she over there dancing with my man.* Keke quickly gathered her things and gave one last look at Pam before storming out of the party. Pam hadn't noticed that she was gone, she was too busy hugging her dance partner. For the next five minutes, Pam and Tyrone were carelessly bumping and grinding on to the latest love songs. By the end of the start of the third song, the two were drenched with sweat and exhausted.

"Let's take a break," he said as he anxiously led Pam off the dance floor. Soon she found herself in a dark corner of the house, everyone around was kissing and touching in the most inappropriate ways. Tyrone had plans to do the same, Pam jumped when she suddenly felt the warmth of his hand running along her inner thigh. He slowly reached for her breast, pulling her close and whispering foul things in her ears. She quickly sobered up, she pushed back up off the wall he had her pinned against and violently shoved his hands off her thighs.

"Don't touch me like that," she shouted frantically.

His touch reminded her of what happened that day at the clinic, a strange man's hand touching her in places he had no permission to. Tyrone wasn't the least phased by Pam's dramatics he was accustomed to women saying no at first.

"Why are you playing hard to get?" he asked taking her hand leading it to his member. She jerked her hand from him once again and they struggled for a moment until she wiggled free.

Pam turned to him yelling at the top of her lungs, "Don't touch me ever again!"

He chuckled while waving her off, a mischievous smirk rested over his lips, "Stop acting crazy girl you know you want me too."

The adrenaline had taken over, Pam wanted to fight him, but her instinct said run, so she took off towards the door pushing past several confused partygoers. She accidentally knocked a cup out of one girl's hand, spilling her strawberry daiquiri all over her white dress. She threw an apology over her shoulder as she scrambled to make her way out of the party. The woman stood frozen, upset about her new dress being ruined. Tyrone made his way over to his new damsel in distress to make his introduction.

Outside Pam found Keke restlessly leaning up against the car trunk. She stood with folded arms and perked lips, impatiently waiting for Pam's return. Keke had stormed out with every intention of leaving, that was until she got outside and realized that Pam was the one who drove them there.

"Keke girl, I am so glad you are still here," breathing a sigh of relief.

"Please Pam, the only reason I am still here is that you drove."

"I am so sorry," Pam pleaded.

"I should have listened to you."

There is so much she wanted to tell her; Pam had no one to talk to about all the things she was feeling. Keke was disinterested at this time and Pam could tell.

"Can we go?" she asked as she stormed around to the passenger side.

"Keke what's wrong, why did you leave?" Pam asked innocently   .

"What's wrong, whats wrong?" she echoed angrily.

"Well Ms. Pam, you were in there feeling up on my crush."

"I was?" Pam asked unawares.

"I danced with a lot of guys which one was he?"

"The one you were just bumping and grinding with PAM!" Keke screeched.

Pam tried to grab her hand, "Look at me Keke, I am sorry I didn't know."

"Sure, you didn't," Keke snatched her hand and shrugged her shoulders.

"That guy is no good," Pam continued.

"He tried to feel me up after I said no, he was a freak, and nothing happened I pushed him away and ran outside."

"Really?"

"Nothing happened, I promise, you have to believe me," she said bowing her head.

Keke was relieved that nothing happened.

"Girl my head is spinning." Pam cried touching her forehead.

Keke smiled, "That's what you get, trying to drink and act like you grown."

"You are in no condition to drive, give me the keys," she reached out and snatched the dangling keys from Pam's hand.

It was true, Pam was in no condition to argue; now that she had calmed down the effects of the liquor began to cause her head to spin again.

"Keke, can you drive, do you even have a license?"

"Watch me," Keke boasted confidently.

The car screeched and jerked all the way home. Keke was a new driver and it showed. She stopped hard at stop lights and smashed the gas whenever the lights turned green. The liquor in Pam's stomach swished around like a washing machine on spin. After thirty long minutes Keke got them home in one piece. That night was the first and last of many things for Pam, she liked the thought of sipping away her troubles but was averse to the vulnerability of doing it in public. Her distrust for the intentions of men was reinforced by Tyrone; he had given her more reason to drink but less to party.

In the space of two years from the unfaithful night at the party, Pam sipped many nights away, graduating from "girly drinks" to hardcore liquor. She went from one drink to the other searching for the one whose arms were strong enough to hold her. Pam's favorite spot became the liquor store on her way home from work.

Chapter Nine

Pam first met Trevor when he was a senior in high school; he hid that fact for a long time. He liked older women and loved hanging out with the older boys playing dice, gambling, and talking smack. Trevor had high hopes of becoming a famous reggae artist one day. The older guys loved to hit on women passing by and had competitions to see who could spit the best game. Trevor studied them like they were his schoolbook, mimicking their lines and mannerisms.

The night he met Pam was the first time he tried his new mack skills. He was nervous, his boys had run off to chase some bootie and he patiently waited for her to come outside the store. He watched as she made her way to the car and then made his move.

I have never seen her around before, what if she not from here. I have to say something to shortie, he thought nervously as he peered in the liquor store window. He decided to go for it, she did talk to him but all he was able to get was her name.

From time to time, he would see her come by the store; he would sometimes initiate small talk but never pressured her for anything more. His boys thought he was going soft, he warned against harassing her, they honored his request but teased him none-the-less.

"Well, Ms. Pam where are you from."

Pam began to warm up to him.

"Me I'm from around the way."

"So, Trevor where are you from, I hear an accent."

"Guess," he replied playfully.

"An island, maybe...well you sound like you could be Jamaican," sounding as if she had just answered the final round of Jeopardy.

"Is that your final answer," he smiled acting like a game show host.

"Yes, you are Jamaican aren't you."

"Me a yardie," he said with a charming thick accent.

The conversation was going well, Trevor wanted to leave her wanting more so he faked an 'important' appointment and acted as if he had to go.

"Well, Ms. Pam it was nice speaking with you, but I have to go now."

She wasn't ready for him to leave, she was just warming up, but it was ok because she had a backup date for the night anyway. She waved bye to Trevor and went into the store to get a bottle.

Trevor had developed a routine; it was as if he were two people. See Trevor had a cousin named Devon, they were the same age and both seniors in high school. The two would hang out after school sometimes so that his aunt and uncle wouldn't suspect that he was getting into trouble. Sometimes Trevor would play ball and other times he would go into the house pretending to do homework. Whenever Devon disappeared to wherever he would go, Trevor took the opportunity to go hang out on the edge of town with his crew the Lion Possie.

Staying out of trouble was the only way to avoid deportation back to the island. Trevor, a senior, had just arrived in America after running with a bad crowd back home. His mother, a widow, had sent him to live with her sister in New York to give him a fresh start. With most of her family having left the island, Trevor's mother hoped he would attend university, but he had different plans.

When he arrived in New York it was summertime, the streets were littered, and the place had a film of dirt over it. He found himself looking for ackee, mango and avocado trees in the neighbor's yard instead he found grass. *Grass, dem people ya mad, you can't eat grass.*

The shock of the new environment made it difficult for him to adjust. Everyone back home had spoken of America like the streets were paved with gold, no such thing. Trevor and Devon were the best of friends when they were children, back then they were more like brothers, unfortunately, time had changed that. They hadn't seen each other in years, at first Devon was excited to hear Trevor was coming to stay with them, this quickly changed once he arrived.

Trevor was two-faced and Devon knew it, whenever he was at home with his Aunt Donna and Uncle Linden, Trevor was a saint or so they thought. He had good reason to pick up his new acting gig, the agreement was that Trevor had to attend and do well at school or go back to the one-room zinc fence house he shared with his mother back home. Even though America wasn't everything they made it out to be, he didn't want to go back to a life of using the outhouse, cooking on Kerosene stoves, and eating flour dumplings and butter every other night.

Since his father's passing, Trevor's life has been a whirlwind of changes. The mystery surrounding his death remains unsolved. Trevor doesn't talk about his father much anymore. He harbors resentment toward him for leaving him and his mother to suffer.

Mama Marie, a market vendor, had to scrape by and sell produce from the country to make ends meet. Trevor was ashamed of their living situation and the fact that his mother couldn't afford to buy him name-brand clothes. He felt like an outsider, with the wealthy youths mocking him. Trevor's frustration turned into aggression, causing multiple complaints from the community about his behavior.

-~-

One scheme that Trevor and some schoolmates developed was during mango season, when Mr. Wilson's tree was loaded with ripe, sweet fruit. Trevor spent weeks plotting, watching as the blossoms turned to flowers, and flowers to young mangoes. Eventually, it was time. He enlisted two fellow schoolmates, Palmer, and Sheldon, to be the lookouts.

The plan was to wait until nightfall when Mr. Wilson and the neighbors were asleep. They would creep out of their homes, sneak into Mr. Wilson's yard, and Trevor would climb the tree to pick the mangoes. Afterward, they would split the bounty, eating some and selling the rest on the road the next day. It almost worked, but they had forgotten about Mr. Wilson's mangy old dog, Willie. Trevor was furious with himself for carelessly scheming about the mangoes and forgetting about Willie.

As planned, Palmer arrived with the basket and Sheldon kept watch. Trevor scaled the tree with ninja-like precision, plucking mangoes as he went. His stomach grumbled, but he resisted the urge to snack, knowing he needed to finish the job. He gathered about twenty juicy fruits, effortlessly dropping them into Palmer's waiting basket. Just as he prepared to climb higher, a faint bark caught his attention. He paused and listened, realizing the sound was getting closer by the second.

"Sheldon, Sheldon," Trevor called in a low pitch voice.

Sheldon looked frightened because the light in Mr. Wilson front porch came on.

"Backside, me gone," Sheldon took off running.

Palmer started to catch him fraid, he claimed he had to get back home. He dropped the basket like it was on fire, shook his head and ran off in the shadow of the night. That left Trevor up in the tree alone, to decide his fate. Willie, the mangy dog, was now barking uncontrollably at the foot of the mango tree. *Shut up dog*, Trevor thought, *you a go get me inna trouble. Dis dog mad, I wonder if me shoulda trow on mango and lik him inna him head.*

He deliberated undecidedly for some time until he heard the voice of his neighbor Mr. Wilson at the base of the tree. He exclaimed while looking at the basket of mangoes, "A whe de ras is dis, who have de nerve fe come inna me yard and pick mi mango dem."

Mr. Wilson scanned the yard, but it was hard to see in the dark. "Come Wille mek we check if di likkle duti thief still de ya," calling the dog to follow him. Willie wouldn't move, he just kept barking feverishly at the mango tree.

"Willie, you gone mad or something?"

Trevor was so nervous that he almost peed on himself. He tried to steady his body so as not to make the tree shake. That was the longest two minutes of his life, and he would have gotten away if the mango that he was in the course of picking before Willie came didn't drop.

Buff! Mr. Wilson swirled around looking straight up in the tree.

"Is who dat, come out now before me get me a machete and chop you up."

Trevor was petrified, he was ready to wave his white flag and surrender.

"No sir Mr. Wilson don't hurt me please, I am the only son for my mother you will break her heart," he pleaded.

"Break her heart nuh, weh you a do up inna me tree ah thief me mango dem?"

"I gwan go show unnu likkle bad breed pickney," he promised.

Wilson, fuming with anger, grabbed young Trevor by the collar and dragged him to his mother's front yard. He pounded on her door and berated Mama Marie about her son's misbehavior. Despite her apologies and pleas, Mr. Wilson refused to listen to her. He continued to rant and rave, still holding Trevor in his grasp. Finally, Mr. Wilson released him, but not before giving him a command.

"You!" he pointed at the young boy, who was relieved to be free.

"Meet me at my house tomorrow morning before school."

The next morning, Trevor arrived bright and early at Mr. Wilson's yard. Surprisingly, the man seemed more composed this time around. He offered Trevor a deal; he would serve one week before and after school for every mango he stole. Since Trevor had taken twenty mangoes, this meant he would work for twenty weeks.

Later that day, he ran into Palmer and Sheldon at school. At the sight of them, he flew into a blind rage. In a fit of anger, he chased them through the courtyard until he caught them in front of the principal's office. Without considering the consequences, he swung at them, missing Sheldon but landing a punch in Palmer's face. The children ran to their teachers to report the fight, and soon Mr. Drumman arrived. He managed to pry Trevor off Palmer and escorted them both to the principal's office.

They reported him to his mother.

Fighting! Suspended from school? What is wrong with you son?" his mother lamented. Mama cried living tears, she did her best but for Trevor, her best wasn't good enough.

Chapter Ten

Trevor quickly became the talk of Valley High. His deep voice, silky Caribbean accent, ebony skin, and good looks made him a hit with the ladies. It was no secret that Trevor enjoyed the attention, and he noticed that Jackie had a soft spot for him. She wasn't exactly his type, but he appreciated the way she made him feel. Whenever Trevor and his cousin Devon were hanging out, Jackie would find a way to be nearby.

Trevor couldn't help but feel a smug satisfaction every time he saw Jackie admiring him from afar. He knew Devon had feelings for her, but that didn't stop Trevor from basking in the attention. It was almost too easy to play up his charms and make Devon feel inadequate.

The stark contrast between their lives was a constant source of pain for him. Devon had his own room, well-off parents, new clothes, and a standard of living that Trevor could only dream of. Strange as it was, he found solace in the fact that the girl his cousin yearned for was attracted to him. It was his twisted way of getting even.

During senior year, Devon and Trevor were relaxing in front of their house when they spotted Jackie walking by. Out of the blue, Devon pointed in Jackie's direction and exclaimed, "There she is!" Devon proceeded to tell Trevor in the earshot of Jackie that Jackie had a 'big ol' crush on him. The next thing that the two of them remember was Jackie taking off full speed down the street. After that weird encounter Trevor didn't see Jackie around for some time well until the note.

"Trevor come ansa the phone," his aunt called from the other room. His mother had called from Jamaica bursting with tears, she was so proud of her boy for graduating some thing she never got a chance to do.

"I'm so proud a you son."

"Thanks mama," he replied.

"Sorry I could't mek it, you know how things stay wid me," he smiled to hide his disappointment.

"Yes mama, I know me a go try fe make it betta one day watch."

"Mek sure you tek care of you self and stay out of trouble, remember seh you are mi one son," she admonished.

Trevor sensed where the congratulatory call was headed. He wanted to cut it short before she began to reminisce and cry once more, so he interjected quickly.

"Mama me nuh wan run out your phone credit, give thanks for calling I will talk to you again soon," he walked back into the kitchen to hand his aunt the phone. Trevor didn't want to be in the house when his aunt got off the line, so he quickly got ready and told her he was going out.

The sun was blazing, the heat too intense to stay inside. With the day still young and nowhere to go, Trevor decided to shoot some hoops. He invited Devon to join him, but he declined, too busy with his upcoming college plans. While Trevor had no college aspirations, he was determined to make it big in reggae music. As he made his way to the court, he spotted a familiar figure – Jackie. It had been a while since he last saw her. Without hesitation, he approached her from behind, hoping to catch her off guard.

"Looking for someone," he said in a seductive tone.

Jackie was startled. They exchanged words and then Jackie told Trevor she had something for him. She reached around in her bag and handed him a sealed envelope with his name on it. Surprised yet anxious to have something to hold over Devon's head, he took the note with a smile.

"Hope to hear from you soon," she said waving as she made her way cheerfully up the street.

Trevor stuffed the note into his gym bag and headed off to play ball. His team lost two games in a row, and he decided to call it quits for the day. As he walked back home, all he could think about was taking a relaxing shower. Upon arriving, he was greeted by the pleasant smell of his aunt's cooking.

"Is that Devon I hear?" Trevor sighed.

"No, Auntie, it's just me - Trevor."

It seemed like everything these days was always revolving around Devon, and he couldn't help but feel irritated by it.

"Oh, Trevor how you do, come here mek me talk to you."

This is the last thing he needed, another long-drawn-out talk. He strolled into the kitchen and took a seat by the bar.

"Yes, Auntie," he braced himself.

"Trevor, your uncle and I are proud of you for graduating school, but as you can see your cousin Devon is going on to college and you haven't applied to one."

"Now that you are getting older, you need to start taking your life more seriously," she pressed.

"Auntie I have told you I am going to be a big-time reggae artist," he said popping his imaginary collar.

"Ah so nuh," she mocked.

"So, tell me something big time reggae artist how you a go eat in the meantime?

"Do you plan on getting a job any time soon?"

Her spitfire questions only frustrated him more.

"Your uncle is going to speak to you later about getting you a job where he works."

What, as a construction worker, ever since his experience with Mr. Wilson back home Trevor had a huge disdain for all things manual labor.

Trevor was seething with anger, but he managed to excuse himself from the conversation with a polite smile. As he walked down the hall, he couldn't help but mutter curses under his breath. He thought about his life, his family, and the source of all his problems – Devon. He needed a plan, something better than the mango plan. He couldn't think straight with this funk rising off his body, so he headed to the bathroom for a long shower to clear his head. When he emerged, he hoped that Devon wasn't back yet because he needed to read the note from Devon's sweetheart in private. First things first.

Trevor entered the room and closed the door behind him. He reached down into his duffle bag, but the first thing he smelled was a pair of dirty socks. It was wet and moldy inside the bag, so he decided to dump everything onto the floor and rummage through it to find what he was looking for. Despite the letter being a bit crushed, it was still legible. Finally, he found it, *Aha, here it is!*

He sat down next to his pile of clothes, resting his back lazily on the bed. He couldn't resist gloating to himself, *let me guess, oh Trevor how I love thee let me count the ways. Ha, I knew that girl had a thing for me since day one. Wait until Devon hears about this.* He opened the letter slowly, flashing it open with one flick of his wrist.

> Hey,
>
> I wanted to say that although you are a nice guy and all, I don't get that vibe from you. Maybe there is another girl out there for you, I hope you find her.
>
> Sincerely,
>
> Jackie

Wah, dis gyal bright and feisty! What kinda foolishness is this? How she a go write to me, Trevor de gal dem suga and tell me seh me should go look for 'another girl out there, he protested. *Devon had done it again. First, he shows off on him and now dry foot Jackie has the nerve to do the same.* The funny thing is, she is not, had not, and will not ever be my type. *Nice guy is this girl serious.*

Trevor's mind raced with conflicting thoughts. He was tempted to confront Jackie and give her a piece of his mind, but at the same time, he didn't want Devon to find out about the letter. Just as he was trying to decide what to do, he heard Devon coming up the stairs. In a panic, he tore up the note and buried it under the laundry pile. Devon knocked on the door, and Trevor grudgingly invited him in.

"What's up, cuz?" Devon greeted him cheerfully.

"Don't forget the upcoming wedding reception in Brooklyn this weekend."

Struggling to keep his composure, Trevor forced a smile and offered a half-hearted response. He made an excuse to leave the room pointing towards the laundry pile on the floor. Trevor gathered up the clothes and hurried downstairs to the basement to plan his next move while doing the washing.

The following day, Trevor stationed himself in front of The Liquor Palace, eagerly anticipating Pam's arrival. It had been days since he last saw her. As he waited in front of the store one of his friends walked up, he noticed that one of his boys was missing.

"What happened to Jay?"

"He got busted for selling weed last night and they took him downtown," he shook his head.

Jail, the thought sent shivers up Trevor's spine. This was the first time any one of the crew got caught up like this, they weren't into anything serious that would warrant jail time, but things were beginning to change.

Trevor was a bundle of nerves, he almost gave up and walked away, but then a candy-red Honda pulled up and parked. He breathed a sigh of relief, "Yes, it's her." He was determined to ask Pam out. He needed two things an ego boost and a date for the wedding reception.

Pam's face lit up when she saw Trevor, but she quickly composed herself, not wanting to appear too eager. The last time they spoke, Trevor had left her hanging, and she was curious to know more about him.

"Hey Pam, how is it going?"

"I'm good Trevor, how are you?"

"Good now that I see you."

"Pam, I have a question for you."

"For me?" She asked, putting her hand over her mouth trying to hide her smile.

"Yeh, what would you say if I invited you to a reception I have to go to this Sunday?"

"Like a date?"

"Yeh, something, like that."

"I am flattered, but" she paused.

"But what? Don't tell me you got a man," he recoiled.

"No, that's not it," she hesitated.

"Pam comes on I have been watching you come here for the last year, I never disrespected you or tried to hurt you. You can trust me."

She thought about what he said, "Give me a minute I am going to run inside and be right back."

He agreed to wait while she made her usual run. When she came back out, he was leaning up against her car. He had an irresistible vibe she couldn't deny, "So what's your answer," he asked again.

"I will meet you there, just give me the address and the

time," teasing him away from her car.

She bent down to open the door got in and placed her bottle in the passenger side; Trevor leaned on the window and said, "Can I ask you one more question?"

"Who is drinking all these bottles you keep buying? Somebody you know must have a real serious drinking problem."

That touched a nerve; Pam politely smiled and changed the subject. "I look forward to seeing you next Sunday, be safe."

"Alright cool," he winked giving the car a tap, "drive safe."

CHAPTER ELEVEN

Pam was delighted to finally be spending time with Trevor; she had never been on a *real* date before. *Relax Pam*, she coached herself as she anticipated going on the date. *You need to get out more and Trevor has been sweating you for a while now.*

She was nervous around, but she reasoned that the wedding was going to be in a public space, and she didn't plan on drinking. *A date, I gotta get something to wear and oh yeh I need my hair done,* she thought remembering what Rita had told her.

"Keke girl I am finally ready for you to do my hair," Pam was giddy and noticeably in a good mood.

"Really," Keke sported.

"Finally, after all this time you."

"Yeh, can you meet me at my house on Sunday morning?

"I have a date."

"Date?" Keke echoed.

She was excited for Pam but leery of whether she could handle herself alone. Keke didn't want to discourage her, so she drummed up some enthusiasm.

"Girl what are you going to wear? I hope not one of the frumpy outfits you call clothes?"

Pam didn't know what she was going to wear; she would need to go shopping for something. She asked Keke to come with her to make sure she got something that would make her look good. Keke suggested they go to the Ave; she said it was a great place to find everything she needed.

Pam bought a hot pink form-fitting knee-length dress, some pink shoes with lime green accessories. This was out of the norm for her, but she wanted to make a good impression on Trevor.

"Girl you are about to be the talk of that party."

"I am going to hook your hair up; your date is not going to be able to stop drooling."

Keke's hair skills had improved since she started working at the shop, but Pam wasn't sure she wanted anything over the top. Pam remembered the ponytail style she gave Rita when they first met, she always wanted to know what she would look like with a little extra weave up top.

"Keke, do you remember that my first hair client Rita who I gave that ponytail style to?"

"Can you do that style?"

"I always like that style; I need you to replicate it to the T, cocked off to the side with a bang swoop and everything."

She laughed clapping her hands together in excitement.

"Oh, everything except the red streak of course," I am going to a wedding, and I don't want to do too much.

-~-

Pam arrived in Brooklyn about nine o'clock that night, Trevor told her to just come on in when she got there, it was a grand celebration, and no one was bothering to check who was who. The party was underway, reggae music was pumping from the stereo system, and people were dancing, drinking, and having a good time.

She anxiously searched around the dimly lit room looking for Trevor, *did he stand me up?* She felt uncomfortable in her outfit; she felt the eyes of all those strangers looking at her. She fidgeted about tugging at the hem of her dress questioning if she made the right choice in agreeing to come.

A ball of nerves welled up in her stomach so she couldn't take it anymore; Pam spun around looking for the sign for the bathroom, there it is all the way across the dance floor and past the DJ booth. Pam rushed across the floor using her hands to part the sea of people; someone grabbed her hand just as she was about to pass the DJ booth. This uninvited touch startled her, she flung her head around to see which stranger had lost his mind tonight.

"Dang Pam, that's you?" Trevor playfully twirled her around while still holding her hand.

"Trevor!" she breathed a sigh of relief.

"I'm so glad I found you there are a lot of people in here, I almost thought to leave," she said pointing to the crowd.

He leaned in so she could hear him over the music, "Leave?"

"I am glad you didn't leave; you look too good tonight."

Pam was flustered; Trevor looked so handsome standing there in his dress clothes, the smell of his cologne made her feel weak.

"Pam, I am going to get a drink do you want one," he pointed towards the bar.

She hesitated for a good few moment contemplating whether she would break her no social drinking rule this once, *why not* she thought *it's been a while.*

"What are you drinking," motioning having a drink with his hands.

"Rum and coke, I always wanted to try that," she giggled.

Trevor smiled as he bopped his way over to the bar, *yeh so de gal Jackie de ya, I didn't even know she knew the bride and dem. What a small world, she was the last person I expected to see tonight, but I sure am glad I invited Pam. I will show her and*

Devon, Trevor counseled himself.

Trevor had more reasons than one to show up tonight, he had long wanted to ask Pam out and now was the best time given that Jackie had the nerve to be her too. He was still sour about the note she had given him, and tonight was payback.

Pam had gone to the restroom to freshen up and was on her way to look for her date when she spotted him by the DJ booth with the drinks.

"Rum and Coke," lets toast he suggested as he lifted his glass to hers.

"Alright," she blushed.

Their eyes locked as the drink glasses touched.

"To a good time," he grinned.

"To a good time," she replied.

Pam spun the ice cubes around in her glass, trying to settle her nerves. She wasn't used to drinking rum and coke, but tonight was different – she wanted to let loose with Trevor. As she sipped the cocktail, the warmth of the alcohol spread through her body, easing her tension and inhibitions.

The music on the dance floor was too loud, so they stepped into a nearby hallway to talk. As they leaned in close to hear each other, Trevor made her laugh with his jokes. Pam's smile drew him in, and he took a chance. In a hushed tone, he whispered in her ear, "Can I kiss you?"

He leaned in and she couldn't help but feel drawn to him. She hesitated for a moment before finally giving in to the kiss. His touch was gentle as he stroked her hair and looked deeply into her eyes. The kiss was passionate and invigorating, and Pam couldn't help but feel like she was in a state of bliss. This was the first time since Chad that a man had made her feel this way. As the emotions flooded over her, she slowly backed away, trying to regain her composure.

"You alright?" he asked, concerned that maybe she didn't

like his kissing.

"No, I am fine," she assured him.

"Let's dance," before he could answer she had pulled him onto the dance floor.

They embraced one another like old flames dancing seductively to a reggae lover's rock selection. Over Pam's shoulder, Trevor could see Devon at Jackie's table, suddenly they both got up making their way to the dance floor.

Look at him dancing like a lame, ha! Oh, so Jackie wants Devon now, she just using him to make me jealous. I am convinced something is wrong with that girl, Trevor mocked.

Trevor looked intently at Jackie waiting for the perfect opportunity to rub his *new girl* in her face. It worked, Jackie saw him, and she looked troubled.

Pam danced the night away enjoying the time she spent with Trevor around twelve o'clock when she realized it was getting late.

"I have to make my way back to Queens," she said during a brief intermission.

"You're right it's getting late," Trevor replied, glancing at his watch.

Without a word, he took Pam's hand and guided her through the crowded dance floor. They exchanged small talk outside.

"Thanks for coming," he said, still holding onto her hand.

"You had a few drinks in there," he noted, impressed at how well she could handle her liquor.

"Are you okay to drive?"

"I'm good," she joked, walking a straight line.

"See? Perfect balance."

"Be careful," he cautioned.

"I don't want anything to happen to you, Ms. Pamela."

The way he pronounced her name was everything, there was something about his accent that she found irresistible. She released his hand and walked away, swaying her hips.

Trevor leaned against the car door, watching as Pam slid into the driver's seat.

"Drive safe," he said, blowing her a kiss and winking his right eye.

"I'll catch up with you later."

The moment Pam drove off, Trevor redirected his attention towards his cousin Devon and Jackie. His bruised ego still demanded revenge. He searched for Devon and found him in the corner trying to impress Jackie. Trevor motioned at his watch and signaled it was time to leave, but Devon wasn't interested in going anywhere. He made several more attempts to get him to leave, but he was brushed off every time. Finally, his patience ran out. He stormed over to the table, the tension thicker than ever.

"Cuz, I don't want to break up your *date*," he mocked using his hands to make parenthesis around the word date.

"But I'm ready to go."

Devon responded cooly, "No prob cuz."

Trevor felt a twinge of irritation at Devon's kindness towards the girl who had previously insulted him. Jackie couldn't help but notice Trevor's odd behavior and grew curious about the mysterious note. Devon went to retrieve the car, leaving Trevor by the door. This was the perfect time for Jackie to get some answers.

"Did you get my note?" she asked, approaching Trevor.

"Yes, and as you can see, I found someone who's right for me," he replied shortly.

"Why are you talking to me now?"

Taken aback by his hostile tone, Jackie stammered, "Let me explain."

Trevor's anger was palpable as he turned towards her, his body language suggesting he was ready to attack.

"Look, girl, I didn't want you. You were always looking at me, and when you finally had something to say, you wrote to reject me," he said, ticking off each fact with his fingers.

"So, you into playing games huh, I see you have been all buddy, buddy with my cousin Mr. Goodie two shoes Devon."

"Well guess what, he is the better man for you anyways because to be my girl, you have to put out!" He said moving his waistline around. Trevor's words cut Jackie like a knife. He spoke at length about Pam's beauty and curves, emphasizing how much he was attracted to her. Jackie was stunned and overwhelmed by Trevor's coldness. She was unable to find the courage to respond to his words, so she remained silent and let him continue.

Trevor stormed out the door, and pushed past Devon, who had just arrived. Jackie watched him leave, feeling heartbroken and confused. The ride home was silent, with Trevor not saying a word to Devon the entire way.

CHAPTER TWELVE

Trevor and Pam's relationship blossomed as they started to spend more and more time together. Pam initially hesitated to take their relationship to the next level, but after many late-night conversations, she finally opened up to the idea of being with Trevor. He never rushed her, and she felt at ease around him, almost like she did with Chad, her ex-boyfriend. He would often surprise her at work, taking her out for lunch and shopping. Sometimes, Pam would invite him over to her apartment for a drink, where they would watch movies, chat about life, and relax.

Pam had a bit too much to drink one night, and she and Trevor found themselves entwined on the rose-colored leather sofa in Pam's mother's fifth-floor apartment. It had been years since Pam had allowed herself to be touched, and she vowed to never let a man hurt her again. Trevor was unaware of her secret vow, and as the night continued, the two lost themselves in the moment.

A few weeks later, a sense of déjà vu swept over her when Pam discovered she was pregnant. This time, however, she was determined to keep her baby, no matter what anyone said. When she finally told Trevor, he was taken aback, but his reaction was subdued and difficult to read.

"Trevor, I am pregnant for you."

"Wah you just seh Pamela?" he exclaimed.

"Yes, we are going to have a baby."

"Wow, really, a baby!"

He knew he was in no position to be a father, but he also knew what it was like not to have one. Holding Pam in his arms, he promised her they would find a way to make it work.

Pam's mother had always been a source of conflict, and it was clear that the next step was for her to go. Trevor agreed, eager to escape the watchful eye of his aunt and uncle. With Devon leaving for college, he would be left alone to deal with their prying questions and disapproving tone.

Trevor and Pam decided they would take care of their baby and live together. While Trevor's family was disappointed, they let him go without putting up a fight. They reminded him that they were there for him if he ever found himself in a jam. And with that, Trevor and Pam were on their own. She continued to work at the beauty salon, while Trevor struggled to find work with just a high school diploma. He spent most of his days gambling for rent outside the liquor store. Soon, arguments over money became more frequent and volitile.

Pam's first pregnancy was an isolating and nerve-wracking experience. Trevor, her partner, was distant and quick to blame others for his problems. Despite his behavior, she refused to let him spoil her dream of becoming a mother. During her prenatal appointments, which she attended alone, the doctor shared vital advice on how she could ensure a healthy pregnancy. Smoke-free, alcohol-free, and stress-free were the three major recommendations. Although smoking wasn't an issue, she struggled with giving up alcohol.

At her next appointment, she wrestled with the guilt of having a drink or two and tried to broach the topic with her doctor.

"No amount of alcohol is safe during pregnancy," he said firmly.

"Have you heard of Alcohol Fetal Syndrome?"

"Alcohol Fetal Syndrome?" Pam repeated in concern.

"Pick up some pamphlets on your way out."

On her way out she stopped by the nurse station, there were a pack of glossy pamphlets on the desk, "I'll read them later," she promised the nurse stuffing a few in her purse.

Pam walked in the door late from work to find Trevor was absent. The fridge was nearly empty, aside from a few containers of three-day-old leftovers. Too tired to cook and with little money for takeout, she opted to eat the remaining pasta. Times were tough; they could barely make rent. Her boss Janet suggested that Pam apply for government assistance for her and the baby, but the thought reminded her of her mother's early struggles.

How was it possible to struggle even when her man was at home? This reality conflicted with how she imagined her life would have been had her parents stayed together. Pam was strongly considering applying for the Women, Infants, and Children Program, at least to ensure they wouldn't have to worry about how they would eat.

Pam reached for the stack of pamphlets in her purse and decided to give them a read. The one about Fetal Alcohol Syndrome (FAS) caught her eye. FAS causes brain damage and growth problems in babies exposed to alcohol during pregnancy.

"Brain damage, growth problems?" she gasped.

"I don't want to cause my baby brain damage."

Pam, girl you must get it together, you can't take another drink during this pregnancy, no matter what!

That night, Pam emptied the liquor cabinet, pouring all the bottles down the drain. She was entirely consumed with the thought of her unborn child, so that for the next few months, she prayed every night, rubbing her belly, and asking the Creator for one thing - a healthy child.

Months later, Pam went into labor after work, but Trevor was nowhere to be found. Janet, from the salon, tried reaching him, but to no avail. They rushed her to the hospital, where she gave birth to a baby boy weighing 7lbs 1 oz. The moment Pam saw him, she knew what to call him - Samuel Brixton, after Trevor's father.

Trevor arrived at the hospital to find Pam and their new son fast asleep. Overwhelmed with emotion, he stared at them, tears streaming down his face. For the first time since he was six years old, Trevor cried. The feeling of having created something so precious that needed his protection and love was sobering. Pam awoke to find him wiping his eyes with a tissue.

"Trevor, you finally made it," she said, barely above a whisper.

"What do you mean, *finally*?" Trevor replied, his mood quickly changing from grateful to indifferent.

"No, I didn't mean anything other than we're glad you're here," Pam said apologetically.

Trevor took offense to her comment and tried to pick a fight, accusing her of being selfish. She had no strength to argue her body was still sore from giving birth. Her child's father stormed out of the room, leaving her alone with their new baby.

"Where are you going, Trevor?" she pleaded.

"I'm going to call my mother if you must know."

He stepped into the hall, to dial Jamaica.

"Mama, guess what!" he beamed.

"What happened, son?"

"Don't worry, Mama, it's good news!"

"What is it, my son?"

"Did you get into college?"

"Better than that, I'm a father now!"

"My woman Pam just had a baby."

There was silence on his mother's end of the line until she burst out.

"Father, for who, Trevor?" the old woman was troubled.

"Mama, my girl Pam just had a baby boy."

"I just wanted you to know. I must go now," he hung up the phone even more aggravated.

Three days later, Pam and the baby were released from the hospital. Trevor called a cab to take them home. As Pam struggled to make her way up the stairs, he carried the baby in his car seat. When they arrived at their studio, they were taken aback by a fluorescent yellow notice flapping in the breeze. It was a disconnection notice from the electric company. He kissed his teeth and tore it violently off the door.

Between paying rent, utilities, and buying food, Pam and Trevor were struggling to make ends meet. Fortunately, the girls from the beauty salon came to the rescue by throwing the new mother an after-birth baby shower. Thanks to their kindness, she was able to get clothes, diapers, and even a crib for baby Samuel. A few days after coming home Trevor started disappearing again. Pam had new priorities that didn't involve tracking down a grown man. Later that month she decided to apply for government assistance; at least with some help she could ensure that she and Samuel were fed. After a few months when Samuel got big enough to sit up Pam asked Janet if she could bring him to work with her, the other girls pitched in as well. Pam's village made it possible for her to get through the difficult times.

Whenever Trevor did decide to show up it was for problems and trouble. One day he walked into the house in a huff, she was folding Samuel's clothes, freshly laundered.

"Pamela, are you cheating on me?"

"What are you talking about, Trevor?" she continued neatly placing the clothes in the basket.

"When was the last time you gave me some?"

"Trevor, please, I have been working hard to take care of our baby. I am exhausted!"

"Exhausted? You better give me some now," Trevor demanded, pushing past her towards their room, disturbing the sleeping baby.

A few weeks later Pam found herself pregnant once again. Trevor had one baby and one on the way he grew desperate to make ends meet, so he began selling weed to make a quick buck. Though he was tired of small-time hustling, his attempt to move up the ladder wasb dangerous. He kept his activities under wraps from Pam.

After their daughter Deja's birth, the temptation to drink became too much to handle. Pam weaned her daughter off breastfeeding at just three months so she could pick up her old habit. Starting with a few sips here and there, she eventually began putting liquor into juice bottles and drinking throughout the day at work and home. Trevor noticed a change in her temperament towards the children and the two would often argue when he was around.

After a few months, Trevor's weed hustling business began to pick up, and he started giving Pam money to take care of the house. Soon, he was balling, and other weed dealers started to take notice. With pressure mounting he knew he had to move his family out of their cramped one-room studio. Finally, they found a three-bedroom rental in Springfield, things were beginning to look up.

Whenever Pam probed Trevor about his income, he remained tight-lipped about his lucrative business. She was curious about how he was suddenly able to provide for their family, but also relieved that they were finally in a stable financial position. One day, while enroute to make a deal upstate, Trevor encountered one of his rival dealers at a gas station. The two got into a verbal then physical altercation, Trevor stomped him out, the gas station attendant called the police. They charged him for assault and issued him 120 days in the county jail.

Pam was devastated to learn that the father of her children would have to spend four months behind bars. She promised to hold down the fort until he returned. Fast forward to April, Trevor was back on the streets, trying to find a new path after his bid. Lockdown taught him that a life of crime and its consequences were not worth it.

Trevor found solace in books while serving time. He read books about historical figures such as Malcolm X and Marcus Garvey, as well as books about Biblical Hebrews and Ancient Egypt. He devoured every book available, and by the time he was released, a new dawn had arrived. Trevor had become *conscious*.

Little did Pam know; Trevor had saved a couple thousand dollars from his hustling days. Upon his return, he proposed a new business venture to Pam - a small bookstore that sold conscious literature, natural products, and a small café. When Pam heard about his idea, she was overjoyed to see the transformation in him. She had been worried sick about him, and their son Samuel asked about his father every day. All Pam could say was, "He'll be back."

Pam broke the news of her third pregnancy in four years to Trevor, a month after his return home. Despite his mother's and others' warnings to slow down, Pam paid no heed. Trevor was a better father figure and partner to her children as compared to her own father.

One day, Trevor visited his aunt to touch base and collect his mail.

"It's good to see you, Trevor!"
"I hope you plan to keep yourself out of trouble."

"Yes, auntie."

"Any mail for me?"

She went to the kitchen drawer and retrieved a stack of letters wrapped in a rubber band.

"Is uncle around?"

"No, he went out."

The two sat in silence for a moment, and then his aunt continued.

"Devon and Jackie are getting married."

Trevor feigned excitement, but inside he was boiling with envy, jealousy, and anger. He quickly made an excuse to leave, citing Pam and the children as his reason for departure. *Who told Auntie I wanted to see Devon and Jackie get married?* He muttered to himself, slamming the door behind him.

The mere mention of her name brought back a flood of emotions, reminding him of his past struggles and failures.

Chapter Thirteen

Pam was in the kitchen cooking dinner.

"Hey Babe, how was your day?" She turned towards the door. Trevor's response made it clear he was not in the best mood.

"Trevor, didn't you hear me greet you?" She put the pasta box down on the counter and walked towards him. Pam tried to kiss him, but he backed away.

"Pam, I'm not in the mood right now." He left her standing in the middle of the floor.

"Not in the mood to say hello, Trevor? Really?"

"What happened?"

"Your mother never taught you any manners?"

"Look woman, don't talk about my mother!" He glared at her over the top of the fridge door. The sound of the beer bottle top hitting the floor let Pam know it was going to be a long night.

"Trevor, you haven't been here for two minutes, and you're already starting problems."

He curled his lip the way he did when he was agitated. Just then, their children, Samuel, and Deja, emerged from the living room. Their favorite cartoon theme song was blasting from the television speakers. This made Trevor even angrier because he had warned Pam against letting the children mess with his stereo, especially when he wasn't home.

"How many times have I told you not to let the children mess with my stuff?" The veins in his neck stood out, and they pulsated when he spoke.

Pam turned off the pot of water on the stove; she knew where this was going. Sadly, they had been there so many times before. Trevor's temper was scotch bonnet pepper hot, and nothing could cool him down but time. Pam slid out of the kitchen towards the children. She ushered them into their room and gently closed the door. After a few minutes, the front door slammed shut and she knew it was safe to finish cooking dinner. By eight-thirty, she had bathed and fed the babies, and they were in bed. Her ankles looked like she had tied water balloons around them. Her body ached, and nothing could relieve the pain like a hot shower and a body rub.

Later that night, around ten, Trevor strolled into the room. He knew he was wrong, but instead of apologizing, he had a habit of trying to start odd conversations. Pam was not in the mood; she turned toward the wall and pulled her blanket over her head. Trevor went to take his bath and came back smelling like her favorite cologne. He knew a few caresses and sweet words would make up for his bad behavior. He slid under the covers and began massaging her back. Without much resistance, she rolled over on her stomach. He reached for the oil and pressed every crick and worry out of Pam's body. She hated how weak he made her. Trevor's touch was the reason they had two babies and one on the way.

"Sorry, babe love," he whispered, gripping her back and rubbing his thumbs against her shoulders.

"Ok," was all she could muster. It was already a long day, and she had no strength to contend with him all night.

He shifted in the bed, sitting up to look at her.

"Pam, get up; I want to talk." She sighed and rolled over to see him staring at her.

"You know my cousin Devon is getting married, right?"

-~-

The day before the wedding, Rita visited her personal stylist, Pam. Rita was extra talkative that day, unable to contain her excitement about the plan to crash Devon and Jackie's wedding. Despite Basil's insistent warnings "not to let anybody know about this", Rita could not help but tell someone. She figured there was no way that Pam would know these people, so she thought her secret was safe.

As a safety precaution, Rita used coded nicknames. Pam called her over to the back, the coconut and passion fruit shampoo smell filled the tiny room.

"Ah, that smells like home," Rita sighed in relief.

Pam used the tips of her fingers to massage the crown of Rita's head.

"Pam, you are the best hair washer. No lie!"

She said that every time she came by the salon, but this time she sounded like she really meant it.

"So, how are things going?"

Pam motioned for Rita to sit up in the chair while she wrapped her head in a towel.

"Things," she hesitated. "Well, they are going great!"

"As a matter of fact, I have a wedding to go to later today, and that's why I am here."

Rita jumped out of the chair, whipping her head around. The towel fell off, but she didn't care. She continued to jest and laugh in a fit of excitement.

Pam chuckled, "Rita, sit please. Didn't you say you have a wedding to attend?"

Rita sat reluctantly and refused to hold her head still. She leaned into Pam, speaking in a boisterous tone, "Pam, I say you have to make me look good!"

"I'll try my best," Pam reached for the blow dryer.

"This must be some wedding, Rita, because you are excited to go."

"Excited?"

"Excited!"

"Pam, I say this wedding is a big deal."

Rita acted as if it was her wedding, which bewildered Pam.

"I see," Pam continued, trying not to sound too inquisitive.

"You seem ecstatic. If I didn't know better, I'd think you were getting married," Pam teased.

Rita leaned forward in the chair, clapping her hands in jubilation.

"Well, you never know."

She confided in Pam about "cutie D,", and his "dry foot" fiancee. Rita claimed that she was the heroine who had to save cutie D from marrying the wrong woman. According to her, if he married his dry foot girlfriend, he would live a lackluster life of boredom.

"Pam, I'm telling you the man wants me; he just doesn't know it yet."

Rita delivered the entire conversation in Jamaican Patois, and, amusingly, Pam understood every word, thanks to Trevor.

"So, guess what," Rita leaned toward Pam and began to whisper.

"When the pastor asks who objects to this union, I am going to walk up there and stop him from making the biggest mistake of his life."

This was getting serious, and Pam was unsure of Rita's plan, but she chose to remain silent. It reminded her of how Chad's mother interfered in their relationship back in high school. Something about the entire thing left a bad taste in her mouth.

"Oh, no time is going. I'm going to be late!"

Rita scrambled to collect her things, thanked and paid Pam, then made her way hurriedly out the door.

However, Rita wasn't the only one with an event to attend that day. Pam had to attend a family gathering with Trevor, so she packed up her things early.

Dry foot gyal. The phrase was all too familiar to Pam. It was the same name that Rita had used to describe the woman whose wedding she was going to break up, and the same word Trevor had used to describe Jackie. As she tried to brush off the thought, she realized that it could just be a coincidence. After all, the city was full of ashy people.

Pam, Trevor, and their children arrived late to the wedding, thanks to her decision to spend half the day at the salon. As they made their way into the room, they could see that it was still filling up. Trevor, not wanting to cause a scene, suggested they sit in the back row. Pam looked at him in disgust. He had been acting strange ever since they received the invitation, and now he didn't even want to sit with his family. This was surprising, given that Trevor was the groom's cousin.

Speaking in hushed tones, Pam leaned in and said, "Trevor, we won't be able to see anything from here. Besides, your family is sitting right over there." He ignored her gesture and led the way, making his way to the back row. Trevor held his son Samuel's hand a little tighter, putting him down in an empty seat. Pam followed behind, reluctantly giving up the argument. In her arms, their beautiful little cinnamon-brown baby girl, Deja, looked like a real-life doll, with her long lashes, thick hair, and sweet smile - she was irresistible. It wasn't long before the woman sitting in front of them noticed them.

"Your babies are precious," she leaned forward, patting Anne's hand.

"Do you mind if I give her a sweetie?" The man with the small afro beside her grew agitated and began to quarrel with her.

"Sit down, will you?" Basil grumbled.

The woman enjoyed the attention, and flirtatiously winked at him. Trevor was put off by her attire, but he accepted the candy and mumbled a thank you. He signaled to Pam to keep a close eye on the children, silently communicating his unease with strangers touching them.

Pam was still annoyed that Trevor insisted they sit at the back. She could barely see beyond the sea of people's heads. As the place began to fill up, the preacher cleared his throat to capture everyone's attention. Trevor clicked his tongue, loud enough for Basil to turn around. Their eyes locked, making Trevor uneasy, but he refused to look away. He slightly cocked his head, as if to say, *Is there a problem?* Basil slowly spun around in his chair, prepared to watch the drama unfold.

Moments later, the crowd erupted in chaos. Pam struggled to comprehend the locals' clamoring. It was difficult to see. Suddenly, the source of the commotion was revealed. "Rita!"

Everything clicked into place. Rita's Cutie D was Trevor's cousin Devon, and the dry-footed girl was Jackie. Pam knew what was coming next — Rita was going to disrupt the ceremony.

Trevor's face twisted into a devilish smirk as he watched the mystery woman create a scene.

"Yes, Devon and Jackie are finally getting what they deserve," he thought to himself. His eyes remained fixed on the altar as the couple disappeared behind the door. However, Trevor's hopes were soon shattered when Devon and Jackie resolved their differences and exchanged vows. He was consumed with anger and left the venue before the reception even began.

They drove home in silence, Pam struggled to process the recent events. Trevor was swerving in and out of traffic, a habit he always resorted to when he was angry. Although Pam was tempted to remind him that the babies were in the car, she decided against it, not wanting to provoke him any further. She glanced over at him; he was scowling and muttering something inaudible. Judging by how he was acting she knew it was best to keep the latest revelation to herself for the time being.

Trevor drove past their apartment.

"Where are we headed?" she waved frantically.

"Mi hungry," he muttered.

She nodded and smiled in agreement. Her stomach was rumbling too. She leaned back in her seat, shifting the seat belt away from her protruding belly. The baby was pressing down on her bladder, and she had been needing a bathroom break since they had left the wedding.

Trevor didn't bother asking Pam what she wanted to eat; instead, he drove to his favorite West Indian restaurant and told her to get the kids. Pam craved the food from the reception, but they had to settle for Dutch Pot on Jamaica Ave. She hoped that her favorite cook was working today, knowing he would make the food just the way she liked it.

"Trevor," she hesitated, tired of him always calling the shots.

"Didn't we just leave all this food at the reception?"

"Mi, know seh you did a go seh something!" he snapped.

"Pam, I told you already, didn't I!"

"Me neva want fe nyam Devon food!"

"Him always ah show off pon me."

Pam's comment irritated Trevor, and he slammed the car door before storming into the restaurant. Pam and the children followed him inside, and she ordered the escovitch fish and festival, while he opted for his favorite curry chicken and white rice. The children enjoyed the patties and coco bread with ginger fruit punch.

As they sat down, Pam excused herself to use the bathroom. Trevor watched her wobble behind the partition and thought, *Dis gyal me a tell you always a get man vex*. The children knew better than to say anything to him when he was in a bad mood, so they sat quietly, waiting for their mother to return.

While in the bathroom, Pam caught a glimpse of herself in the mirror. She didn't look anything like the woman she was just a few years ago. Her midsection was three times larger, and frown lines etched along the corner of her mouth. Life with Trevor had been stressful. Her only source of joy was her children.

Pam emerged from the bathroom to find Trevor already eating, halfway through his meal. Whatever he was eating must have had a positive effect on his mood, as he was in a much better place. "Hey babes, this food is good," he said, pointing to Pam's plate, even passing her a napkin. Pam smiled and wiped the crumbs off the children's faces.

"Did you see the girl in the white?" Trevor spoke, tearing the last piece of meat off the chicken bone.

Pam realized this was the right opportunity to reveal to Trevor that she knew the identity of the mystery woman. With a nervous laugh, Pam spoke up.

"The woman in the white dress," she paused to get Trevor's attention. "Her name is Rita, and she is one of my clients."

He was now very interested in what Pam had to say. This news was great, as it meant he could finally get a leg up on Devon.

"Are you serious, Pam?" he leaned forward in his chair, a piece of bread hanging from his beard.

"I didn't realize the people she was talking about were your cousin and Jackie."

"What a small world," Trevor chuckled, as he turned the information over in his head. If he could piece it all together, then Jackie and Devon would finally pay.

Chapter Fourteen

Pam divulged every detail she knew about Rita to Trevor and promised to arrange a meeting. Eager to gather as much information as possible, he was willing to do whatever it took. Rita visited the salon later that week, but she was uncharacteristically reserved. Pam pondered whether to inform Rita of Trevor's presence, ultimately deciding against it.

"How are you feeling, Rita?"

Pam inquired while preparing the new hair color.

"Did everything go as planned?"

"No." Rita's curt response revealed a profound sense of despair.

"I understand if you don't feel like talking," Pam replied as she continued styling Rita's hair.

Rita sat in silence, gazing at her phone, and sighing heavily.

"Do you know a girl named Jackie?" Pam brushed Rita's hair, placing it in the washing basin.

The name caught Rita off guard and snapped her out of her reverie.

"It depends," Rita replied.

"Well, I know someone who thinks they know her. In fact, they'd like to meet you and chat."

"Hmm," Rita was intrigued by the offer. Her father had demanded that she redeem herself after the botched attempt, and this might be her opportunity to get back at Jackie.

Rita applied her lip gloss and earrings, "Tell me more," she asked.

Pam replied, "Well, he's, my fiancé."

Fiancé? Why didn't you tell me?"

Pam shrugged, "His cousin is now married to Jackie."

Rita's mood brightened, "You mean to tell me Devon is your fiancé's cousin? What a small world! My prayers have been answered!"

Rita burst into an impromptu praise dance, stomping, and dipping as she sang.

Pam tried to hold in her laughter at Rita's antics, "Let's meet tomorrow and discuss it further."

"Tomorrow it is," she rejoiced hugging Pam in gratitude.

The following day, Rita agreed to meet them at the same coffee shop where her father had scolded her just a few days earlier. They sat in the same booth and discussed their mutual adversary, Jackie, with Trevor employing his island charm to get Rita to spill the beans. Desperate and aware that this was her last opportunity to execute the plan, Rita revealed the details of the scheme and the money involved. She even offered Trevor five thousand dollars to assist her in accomplishing her goal.

As Pam and Trevor walked home, they were in shock with the information they had just learned. Despite their disbelief, they were even more surprised to find out the amount of money Devon and Jackie would inherit if the two didn't stop them. Although Rita seemed genuine, Trevor was still skeptical. To ensure the authenticity of her character, he hired a few guys from his crew to trail her and her father.

Several weeks passed with no updates until Trevor asked Pam to check court records on Mr. Carleton, Basil Thompson, his wife, and Devon. There wasn't much information on Mr. Carleton, Basil had an extensive list of lawsuits, debts owed, and liens pending. Trevor realized that he could potentially earn more than five thousand dollars if he made a deal with Devon. His guys eventually came back with pictures and evidence confirming that Basil Thompson was indeed a crook.

-~-

Trevor was lounging on the couch in his boxers when Devon arrived. He had asked him to come over, claiming that it had been a while since they last hung out. The atmosphere in the apartment was tense, reminiscent of a gangster movie. Devon stood by the door, scanning the room for a suitable spot to sit.

"Hey, Cuz, have a seat," Trevor urged.

"By the way, congrats! I'm glad you and Jackie are finally married." He forced a smile and a nod of approval.

"Yeah, thanks, man, what's up?

"How have you been?"

"Good, everything is good." Devon sensed the tension and waited for Trevor to get to the point.

"You're like a brother to me, Cuz," Trevor said.

"Brother?"

"I have some news to share. Have a seat."

Trevor divulged the details about Basil, Rita, and their plan. He explained that with his help, Devon could get rid of them for good. The only catch was that Devon would have to give him a "thank you" gift for his assistance.

"A thank you gift?"

So, this was the real reason for their meeting.

"Fifteen thousand dollars wouldn't hurt."

Devon was stunned. First, he found out that Basil was a crook after all, plus, his own cousin was sticking him up for fifteen thousand dollars just to "help him" straighten everything out.

"Oh, and by the way, you can't tell Jackie."

What? Another secret? Although he was upset, Devon remained calm and collected, listening to Trevor's every word.

"Wow, it's already nine o'clock," Devon stretched and stood up from his seat. He leaned in to give his cousin a goodbye handshake.

"Thanks for the intel, Cuz. I'll be in touch for sure." He made his way toward the door as quickly as possible.

"Make sure you keep me updated."

"Remember, time is of the essence."

Devon made his way home in silence, his mind in overdrive after the recent turn of events. What began as an unexpected inheritance from his old friend, Mr. Carleton, had spiraled into a complex web of deceit and betrayal. *Was it Basil Thompson who schemed the wedding drama surrounding Rita? And was his cousin Trevor's offer of help just a facade for extortion?*

Devon rode home in silence wishing Mr. Carleton was alive so that all this mess could be resolved. He parked his car in front of their new house and contemplated the decision he had to make. *Should he break his vow to Jackie for her own good, or tell her and let the chips fall where they may?*

Island Twist
Book Three
Basil & Rita

Chapter One

Basil Thompson fidgeted in his seat, barely able to contain his excitement. He sat in the third row, neck craned forward, anticipating the start of the event. Next to him, a heavyset woman in a push-up bra and a pearl necklace jostled him with each passing guest, causing Basil to shift uncomfortably in his seat. He dabbed his forehead with an Armani silk handkerchief, gifted to him by a satisfied client. The thick scent of Egyptian Musk and shea butter hung in the air, surrounding him.

Earlier that day, he had visited his barber, Jay, who gave him a clean shave for the occasion. He grinned cheekily, asking Jay to make him look sharp. After a half-hour session, Jay handed him the mirror, and Basil was delighted with the outcome. He was still contemplating wearing his favorite hat, but everything had to go perfectly.

Upon arriving at the venue early, Basil chuckled to himself, *the early bird catches the worm.* He inspected the event hall, taking mental notes of each detail. Once satisfied, he secured the best seat in the room, waiting anxiously for his plus one to arrive. The room slowly filled up with guests, his head swiveled back and forth, checking the door and his watch.

"She needs to hurry up!"

Basil struggled with his conscience; he knew that he had no choice but to go through with the plan.

I deserve this more than anyone else, and I won't let them take it away from me. He refused to take accountability and needed someone else to blame. *This is all Rita's fault. Just like her mother, all beauty, and no brains.* His uttering caught the attention of the woman sitting beside him, Ms. Push up, who leaned in assuming he was talking to her.

Basil was unimpressed, kissing his teeth and shifting in his chair. *This is all Mr. Carleton's fault*, he continued, blaming the *miserable old man* for changing everything at the last minute. The lawyer shook his head silently in agreement with himself. Twenty minutes passed and there was still no sign of Rita, so he continued to look around the venue taking inventory. He observed the crystal streamers falling elegantly from the ceiling, the glitter on the floor, and the centerpiece and silk tablecloth.

"So, this is what they're spending my money on," he muttered in disgust, reaching for the program tucked away in the seat pocket in front of him. His eyebrows rose and fell with each inspection, taking in every detail with a critical eye.

The wedding was set to begin at four, but the ceremony had yet to start because everyone was running later. Beside him, his admirer watched as he fidgeted with his phone, cursing Rita under his breath. The wedding hall hummed with chatter as it filled up.

"So, Jackie and Devon are going all out. Three-course meal, swag bag, Devon is mistaken if he thinks he'll spend all my money!" Basil whispered to his companion.

"She better not disappoint me, or else she's going back," he continued, his tone icy.

Finally, at ten to five, Jackie and her father appeared at the top of the aisle, signaling the start of the ceremony. Basil snarled at the bride, "showtime," he said sarcastically. He was not here to see "that gyal Jackie," who was, in fact, a big part of the problem that he was trying to fix.

The room collectively gasped as the beautiful bride made her way down the aisle, her soon-to-be-husband, Devon, bursting with anticipation as she approached. He wore a welcoming smile, his eyes growing misty with tears. He had been waiting for this moment since they first met, and as fate would have it, their lives would be woven into a beautiful tapestry of love.

Jackie had always followed the rules, and today was no exception. As she walked down the aisle, her father by her side, she locked eyes with her partner waiting for her at the altar. Although Jackie was nervous, she was ready to exchange vows. Suddenly, a commotion broke out in the back of the hall, interrupting the ceremony. The guests' attention was diverted, and everyone turned towards the back of the room.

Basil leaned over to the well-endowed woman and whispered, "Who is she?" His question echoed throughout the room as the woman repeated it. She pointed towards the runway and exclaimed, "Who is she?" Rita was ready for her big moment, and her father was confident that it would be a performance to remember.

As the woman sauntered up the aisle in her fitted white dress, red stilettos and tiara, the entire room watched. Her father subtly winked at her as she passed him, giving her the green light and boosting her confidence to execute their plan. The graceful sway of her hips caught everyone's attention, and they waited in anticipation to see what she would do next. Rita kept reminding herself of her worth, repeating, "I am wife material, not her."

"Rita!" they exclaimed.

A woman from the back row with a large bust shouted, "What kind of mix-up is this?!" while another person balked. Jackie looked to Devon for guidance. They both had reason to fear whatever Rita had to say - Devon because of the note and Jackie because of the phone call.

Suddenly, Devon sprang into action, clasped Jackie's arm, and whisked her away to a nearby room. Rita was left standing at the altar alone, but that was the plan. The scene she caused sent whispers through the crowd, and Jackie and Devon were sure to break up. Rita looked over at the bride's section - Mama was scowling, and Jackie's family looked on in disgust. That didn't stop Rita, though; she brazenly made her way over and took a seat.

The bride's family was troubled by Rita's presence, and even more bothered by the fact that their daughter and soon-to-be son-in-law had disappeared into the back room. Mama was growing increasingly agitated. Jazz, Jackie's brother, leaned forward to tap Rita on the shoulder.

"Miss, who are you, why are you sitting here, and what do you want?" he demanded.

She was in a daze, giddy with excitement, so she didn't hear him at first.

"Miss!" he yelled. Rita whipped her head around in such a hurry that she scrambled to catch her tiara.

"What is it, sir? Can't you see I'm getting ready to marry my first love?"

"What is this madwoman talking about?" he responded brashly.

"I tapped you, lady, because you're sitting in my sister's seat. "Now please see your way to the back!"

Rita let out a menacing laugh. "Sister, which sister?" she jeered.

"Look, lady, are you going to leave, or am I going to have to help you leave?" he asked, standing up. His twin brother was trying to calm him down, but Jazz had a bit of a temper, and it wasn't working.

"Jazz!" A stern voice pierced the tension. It was his father. Jazz knew that he needed to chill out, so he reluctantly took a seat. Rita snickered as she turned around in her chair to face Jazz's direction.

"Me nah move till me get weh me come fa!" With that declaration, she stood up so she could adjust her dress. Rita shamelessly spun around to give everyone a full view of her body. When she was sure Jazz was watching, she winked, blew him a kiss, and slowly sat down again.

"This woman is crazy!" Mama cried in disbelief. Dada held her hand, pressing firmly to signal for her to calm down.

"Let her sit," he advised.

"We don't want to cause a scene on Jackie's big day."

"Yeh, let me sit here. You don't want your precious Jackie's wedding to be ruined," she mocked, finally deciding to turn around in her seat.

Jazz wanted to tell the rude woman a thing or two, but he had to let her insults slide. A good fifteen minutes passed, and still no sign of the bride and groom. The minister ran back and forth trying to keep order. Rita called the minister over to ask if he wasn't going to check on them. He brushed her off after noticing that the caterer had arrived.

The smell of curry, rice, plantains, black cake, and sorrel filled the air. Soon, the people began complaining of hunger. The minister was in the back, pacing the floor, waiting to perform the wedding. Basil just had to know what was happening, so he slid out of his seat and approached the minister.

"Excuse me," he paused for the minister to say his name.

"Minister Jacob," he replied.

"Well, I hope everything is alright."

Minister Jacob's face was riddled with uncertainty.

"Maybe you should check on the couple again."

He agreed and walked gingerly towards the room where the couple had taken refuge. Basil watched until he disappeared inside. Mama's friend Delores was seated in the back too. She was a bit salty about the arrangements and quickly grew tired of the charades. Without hesitation, she made her way to the side door to laywait the minister.

He stepped out of the room after a minute, drawing everyone's attention to him. Oblivious to her presence, he made his way to the front. "Thank you for your patience. The couple will be out shortly," he announced, signaling to Sadie, Devon's cousin, to sing another song.

Delores was inquisitive. She trailed the minister along the wall to the back of the hall, where Basil was waiting for him. Before he could inquire about Devon and Jackie, Delores tapped the minister on the shoulder.

As he spun around, his gaze fell upon the slender woman standing behind him. A lustful look crossed his face, and he signaled to Basil, *excuse me.*

"Yes, ma'am," he asked, clearing his throat, and adjusting his collar.

"Good day, mister preacher man. Excuse me, but is the couple all right?" Delores asked, extending her hand.

"Yes, Ms." the minister hesitated, waiting for her to introduce herself.

"Just 'miss,' sir. My name is Delores," she said, grasping his hand.

She leaned in close, cutting him off mid-sentence.

"The food smells amazing, Minister Jacob. I'm famished."

"Are you hungry too?"

"Is there anything you could do to speed up the ceremony?" Delores purred, brushing her arm against his.

"Jackie is a dear friend's daughter, and I'm getting worried. She and Devon have been in that room for quite some time," she continued, not allowing him to respond.

"I wonder if the delay has anything to do with that fast-tail girl sitting in the front row?"

"You never know. I've seen it all," he replied, letting out a nervous chuckle.

CHAPTER TWO

Esq. Basil Thompson and his daughter Rita had managed to pull off the impossible. They broke up Jackie and Devon's marriage on their wedding day, leaving the home team on the ropes. The pair had spent a while in the room, and by the looks of it the job was almost complete.

Rita was grinning from ear to ear by the time Devon finally emerged. He was furious, and disappointment was evident in his eyes. There were whispers, and then a sudden hush fell over the room when everyone realized that he was standing at the microphone.

Basil perked up, leaning forward in anticipation of the long-awaited announcement. Devon called Rita up to stand with him, and Basil couldn't have been prouder of his handiwork.

"The plan worked! We're in the money now! Retirement, here I come!" he rejoiced.

It was like a scene from a soap opera, and the tension was palpable. Jackie watched from the doorway and soon found herself right beside Devon, who was standing right next to Rita. The rest was a bit of a blur. Jackie attempted to make a confession, but Devon revealed the way in which Rita had tried to trap and blackmail him. It was at that moment that Basil knew the jig was up. He tapped his neighbor and asked, "Can you tell me where the bathroom is?"

Basil hurried past everyone, apologizing as he made his way down the aisle. Once there, he looked back at Rita, who was up front drowning, and decided it was time to leave. Devon had let go of her hand, and now she was exposed. Basil headed to the back door, passing the bathroom on his way out.

Rita searched the crowd for her father, hoping for guidance on the next steps. From the corner of her eye, she saw a shadowy figure slipping out the back door. She was now alone, left to deal with the plan he had concocted. Despite the difficulties of walking down the aisle, Rita refused to give up. She swayed her hips from side to side, head held high, and cried out, "I am wife material!"

Before long, Rita was outside, scanning the area for her father. He had to be nearby since he had only just left a few moments earlier. Her high heels were causing unbearable pain, so she kicked them off and walked barefoot down the street. Passersby pointed and laughed, but she didn't care. The shoes had been rubbing her left baby toe so vigorously that she thought it might pop. After a few more steps, the pain became too much to bear, and she had to stop. She leaned against a graffitied mailbox stationed on the corner, wondering where her father could be.

Rita couldn't believe that he had left her earlier. She scanned the block for any signs of him and spotted someone who looked familiar out of the corner of her eye. He was sitting in a window booth in a small cafe in the middle of the block, reading a newspaper. Eventually, he lowered the paper to take a sip from his cup, and Rita recognized him.

"So, him over there drinking coffee while I'm getting humiliated!"

Despite her throbbing feet, she squeezed them back into the shoes that no longer fit. Adjusting her dress, she hobbled into the cafe and silently took a seat at his table. Basil lowered his paper just enough for his beady eyes to peer over the top. He was not pleased to see her and kissed his teeth.

"Hours of planning down the drain," he grunted.

"Years, me seh years of planning on how to get Mr. Carleton's money only to have you sheg it up at the last minute."

Basil complained about her as if she wasn't sitting right in front of him.

"Plane ticket, housing, food, me even give di gyal a job. All she had to do was break dem up, but no she couldn't even do that right."

"Hours of planning and thousands of dollars down the drain!"

Basil slammed the paper down, causing his coffee to nearly spill over. Rita trembled as her heart raced in fear of what he would do next but was somewhat relieved because they were in public. It was the first time she had ever seen her father so upset. A hint of red seeped into the corner of his eyes as he glared at his daughter. Rita attempted to stand up, but he pulled her back down into her seat.

He spoke in a low raspy tone as he addressed her.

"Your mother told me about your behavior back home."

"Isn't it true that you're the man dem suga?" he asked, looking for a reaction.

She sat silently, with half-closed eyes weighed down by her fake lashes.

"I brought you here to provide you with an opportunity to improve your life," he said, recounting Rita's shortcomings.

Her silence vexed him more, he reached over slapping her hand away from her chin.

"Rita, Rita, do you know how long I've worked on this plan?" She remained silent, aware that he didn't expect a reply.

"Years," he exclaimed so loudly that a waitress rushed to their table, concerned.

"Is everything okay?" she asked nervously, glancing between Basil and Rita.

"We're fine," Basil replied, waving her away. The waitress, whose name tag was obscured by her braids, looked at Rita, who avoided eye contact.

"Is there a problem, Ms. Ke or Kay, whatever your name is?" Basil snapped.

"I'm having a discussion with my daughter. Mind your business."

The waitress hesitated before retreating to inform her manager of the situation at table nine. Basil's anger now focused solely on Rita, but he spoke more softly this time.

"Ms. Island Gyal, all you had to do was convince the man to leave his woman. How hard could that have been? And yet, here we are," he said with a sigh, leaning back in his chair.

She fought back tears, unwilling to show weakness in front of her father. As he continued to berate her, she drifted away, visualizing the soothing sounds of the waves lapping against the shore, she imagined that she was back home.

Chapter Three

Basil slammed $2.45 on the table, jolting Rita out of her reverie. He demanded that they leave immediately, and she struggled to stand up, her feet throbbing with pain. The waitress observed the situation from the back, enlisting her coworkers to assess whether the girl was in any danger. When the manager intervened, everyone returned to their work.

The car ride home was silent, save for the sound of the traffic outside. Rita turned away from her father and gazed out the window, trying to avoid any more conversation with him. As they arrived at her apartment, Basil broke the silence: "Don't be late for work tomorrow. This is not over. I will have to do some big planning to fix the mess you made."

Rita rolled her eyes and mumbled an unenthusiastic reply. She took her time gathering her things, not bothering to put on her shoes. Basil grew impatient and yelled at her to close the door. As she turned around, she looked at him with a heart full of shame and disgust for the man she once called her father.

"Yes Sir, Mr. Thompson," she replied before slamming the car door shut. She waved goodbye dismissively and he drove away.

She lived in a small apartment above Mrs. Hattie, who was unaware that Basil was her father. He had negotiated the deal and promised that Rita would help Ms. Hattie as she was getting old. Mrs. Hattie had just finished making tea when she heard Basil's car pull up. Curious as to why Rita was taking so long, she crept towards the window and overheard the conversation. It was the first time she had heard a different side of the man she thought she knew.

Rita limped her way up the sidewalk and onto her stoop. She knew she still had one more obstacle to overcome before she could get inside and relax: Mrs. Hattie. Gazing up at the brownstone steps, she felt defeated. She dropped her shoes on the sidewalk and sat on the front stoop, her white dress and tiara in disarray. Tears streamed down her face, smudging her heavily powdered foundation. It wasn't just the events of the day that had upset her; it was the culmination of years of pain caused by her father and mother.

-~-

Rita grew up as an only child in Jamaica, raised by her mother Anne. Anne was a twenty-one-year-old university student when she became pregnant by Basil Thompson, a forty-year-old lawyer. When they met, Anne was working part-time at the MoBay hotel. Basil was on vacation and was instantly smitten with Anne, so he asked her to dinner. She accepted, and they spent their first week together in paradise.

Basil was charming and attentive to Anne's every need, and they enjoyed long walks on the beach and hours of conversation. Anne was impressed by Basil's maturity, which distinguished him from the young island boys she was used to dealing with. Furthermore, the fact that he was a lawyer who lived abroad made him even more attractive.

Anne was unaware of Basil's marital status. Basil's wife was his high school sweetheart, and they both studied law at the university. Despite their shared interests, they had a difficult time getting along because they were two sides of the same coin.

Basil hated seeing himself in others. In his world, he was the only one who got to be overbearing, manipulative, and callous. So, he convinced his wife that he needed to take a trip back home and promised that things would be different when he returned.

Anne was a breath of fresh air for Basil. She was young, malleable, and gullible, just the way he liked them. Basil was thrilled with the fact that Anne was so easy to manipulate and control. He felt confident that he could cope with his wife's difficult personality by taking a few trips to the island each year to see Anne.

The first trip ended with a promise to return. Basil left the island with a new muse on his mind. During their long talks, he had filled Anne's head with ideas of moving to America and becoming an artist. To secure his investment, Basil made Anne promise not to *give up the honey pot to any of the likkle duti island bwoy dem.* He was a lawyer, and for him, it was all about contracts. With a little persuasion, Anne agreed to his request.

Chapter Four

Basil returned to Jamaica after three months, just as he had promised. The two picked up right where they had left off, with Basil taking Anne dancing, liming on the beach, and exploring the island's cuisine. Throughout the two weeks, he refrained from making advances towards her. Anne was left curious about the man Basil Thompson really was.

On the last night of the trip, Basil suggested Anne stay over and called her at home around three in the afternoon to confirm.

"Hey Anne, I can't wait to see you."

"Are you packing your bag like we discussed?"

"Yes, Basil," she replied coyly.

"Well, I was thinking we can get dinner at the hotel and go dancing after."

He continued, "It's my last night here and I won't see you for a while so I wanted to spend all the time I can with my Anne."

Anne, the youngest of eleven, lived with her aging parents. Cutting her conversation with Basil short, she dashed to the kitchen as soon as she heard the front door open. Her parents had just returned from the doctor's office.

"How did everything go?" she asked, nervously grabbing a dishcloth to wipe off the stove.

"Everything's fine, my dear," they replied dotingly.

"Can I get you anything to drink?"

"No, thank you. We'll just change and rest for a while."

Anne nodded approvingly and excused herself. She needed to pack for her cover story before it was too late.

Hours later, she emerged from her room with a bag in tow. Her parents were enjoying tea, biscuits, and the evening news on the radio.

"Mom, Dad, I'm spending the night with a friend from work at the hotel. I have the morning shift tomorrow, so I'll go straight to work from there."

"Which friend is that?" her mother asked, arching an eyebrow in suspicion.

"Just a colleague," Anne replied, waving goodbye.

She didn't want to answer any more questions, so she bolted out the door.

-~-

When Anne arrived at the hotel, Basil had a sudden change of plans for their last night together. Upon meeting her in the lobby, he led her to room 203. After motioning her to step back, he opened the door and carried Anne over the threshold, showering her with attention. His affectionate gestures made her feel giddy with excitement.

Basil's lips dripped with sweet words of concern, "Anne, there has been a change of plans."

"Fix your face dear," he continued, "all I wanted to say is that I figured we could call room service over instead of going out tonight."

He took her hand and led her to the bathroom suite, where he suggested she take a dip in the jacuzzi while they waited. Anne's mind was racing with thoughts about Basil's intentions. *Was this a setup? Would he try to take advantage of her and then leave?* She was still untouched and had no intention of being with anyone. However, she couldn't deny that Basil was the best prospect she had come across so far; he was a lawyer who lived abroad and could take care of her if needed.

Anne decided to accept Basil's invitation to use the Jacuzzi. She took her time gathering her night clothes before heading to the bathroom, surprised that Basil did not follow, she considered locking the door while she bathed. Basil cast a discreet glance her way while muttering to himself quietly, "di gyal look good." His goal was to earn her trust, and that required a lot of patience.

She eased herself into the Jacuzzi, and the experience was exhilarating, as it was her very first time. Basil had made all the necessary preparations, turning on the bubbles and the heat. A glass of wine sat next to the tub. The water's warmth and the massage's power worked in tandem, the tension that had built up in her back slowly melted away, a soft moan escaped from her lips. He waited outside the bathroom, he pressed his ears against the door, listening to the water running as she washed off. The scent of steam, lotion and perfume wafted out from beneath the closed door. Though he longed to call her name, he refrained. When she emerged from the bath, Basil was lounging on the bed, appearing as if he had been there all along.

She gathered her clothes and neatly laid them aside. Uncertain of what to do next, she headed towards the peach and green wicker armchair next to the bed.

"No, no my dear Island flower, please sit here, I won't bite." Basil gestured towards the bed and smiled harmlessly.

Anne sat down, her mind racing with thoughts of countless conversations with her girlfriends. She tried to make sense of Basil's strange behavior by discussing it with her friends but none of them had any idea. Anne was so desperate for answers that she even asked her co-worker and friend Buju for advice. He jokingly replied, "Basil is just playing games. If I were him, I would have made a move on you a long time ago."

She stiffened her body in anticipation of his next move and jumped when Basil tapped her shoulder.

"Relax, dear. Here's the menu. Choose what you'd like, and I'll order it for us."

Anne took the menu and quietly perused it. She chose her favorite Escovitch fish and bammi, but Basil corrected her pronunciation and questioned her decision to order something that would make the room smell.

Momentarily second-guessing herself, Anne asked Basil for his suggestion, and he selected brown stew chicken with rice and plantain for both. Taking charge of the situation, Basil's assertiveness didn't bother Anne. She had more pressing concerns, such as whether something was wrong with her and why she and Basil had yet to kiss.

A knock on the door interrupted their conversation. Room service had arrived, and Anne recognized Buju's voice. She didn't want him to see her in her nightwear, so she hid her face until Basil closed the door. The aroma of the food filled the air, and they began to eat, the only sounds being the clinking of utensils and Basil chomping on his salad.

"How was it?" he inquired, observing as she wiped her mouth with a pristine cotton napkin.

"It was really good," she responded, attempting to suppress a burp that trying to embarrass her in front of her man.

Basil extended his arm to collect her plate and positioned it back on the room service cart. He then removed the soiled dishes and shut the door on his way in. Anne couldn't help but notice his muscles bulging through his ribbed T-shirt. Though he detected her admiring gaze, he chose to ignore it. He excused himself and went to the bathroom to freshen up.

Basil gazed at his reflection in the mirror, *Ol' boy, you've done it again. Look at the island girl, she wants me bad.* He prepared himself for the night ahead, stretching and doing a few pushups. "By the end of the night, she'll be begging me for more," he boasted. After his personal pep rally, Basil returned to his room, ready to conquer the night.

Anne lay down on the bed nervously, like a deer waiting for a predator at the water's edge. Basil lay on the far end of the bed, having put a safe distance between them before bidding her goodnight. Thoughts of uncertainty filled Anne's head, and she tossed and turned to find a comfortable position to rest. She had been lying awake for two hours since they had gone to bed, and it was now almost midnight. *Basil hasn't even tried to touch me once,* Anne thought to herself, unsure whether to feel safe or rejected.

While Anne was attracted to Basil, she couldn't shake the feeling that their age difference was a hindrance for him. The anticipation of what might come next was torturous, prompting Anne to break the silence, "Basil," she whispered. At first, Basil feigned sleep and didn't respond.

"Basil," she continued rubbing her long smooth legs up against his.

His eyes shot open, *It's showtime, ol' bwoy.*

Basil could barely contain his excitement, but he didn't want to reveal it just yet. He wanted Anne to beg for what he had in store for her. A small yawn escaped him, as he turned over.

"What's going on, Anne? Everything okay?"

Anne leaned towards Basil's side of the bed, her hand gently stroking his black beard with salt highlights. Basil interpreted Anne's gesture as an invitation to come inside and deliver the package. Anne, on the other hand, was overwhelmed with mixed emotions. He was too preoccupied exploring her to notice. She had never experienced anything like this before and was struggling to tell him to stop. In the end, the tokens of his explorations were scattered on the sheets.

"What's dis?" he asked, running his hands over the hotel bed. Basil leaned over Anne, who was curled up in a ball, to switch on the bedside lamp. He was surprised to find the sheets were stained with a bright red color of innocence. However, this discovery put an extra spring in his step. Anne presented him with flowers, which he considered a victory for a middle-aged lawyer in a stale loveless marriage.

The following day, he hopped on the plane and flew back home, leaving Anne with his work phone as a sign of trust. Four weeks after Basil's trip to Anne's flower shop, he received a call on his office phone - he was going to become a father once more.

Chapter Five

Basil's wife, Claudette, was completely unaware of the child he had conceived outside of their marriage. For twenty years, he provided for his daughter and her mother discreetly, sending a monthly allowance and occasional food supplies to Anne and Rita. Basil's actions were not out of philanthropy, but rather to maintain his own peace of mind.

Initially, when Anne shared the news of her pregnancy with Basil, he reacted by denying any involvement. For Basil, his time with Anne was a fling, a release, and a respite from his stressful life in America. Now, he was facing the responsibility of being a father all over again.

Anne's pregnancy was becoming harder to conceal, and although her parents were disappointed, they were committed to providing support. They took it upon themselves to hold Basil accountable and utilized their network of friends in America to locate him through his phone number. To their surprise, he was a lawyer residing in Queens with a spouse and five children. Basil had little choice but to comply when Anne's parents threatened to contact his wife Claudette if he didn't do the right thing. He doubted their threat for the first few months, but when his wife returned home from church with a message, he knew that Anne's family had followed through on their promise.

"I feel like you're hiding something from me, Basil," Claudette insisted.

She had just returned home from church, her lavender felt hat still pinned to her head. Sister Freda had given her a message during the service, and Claudette was flustered by it.

"Sister Freda said she had a word for me," she began. "Before I could say anything else, she prophesied over me, saying she sees another baby is in the picture. A girl child."

"Basil, we haven't been together in almost two years," she continued.

"I know things have been tough between us, but a baby?"

"I'm not sure Sister Freda is seeing things clearly," Basil replied.

"Who did you say gave the word?"

"Sister Freda," he scoffed.

"You know she's not quite right in the head."

But Claudette wasn't convinced by Basil's dismissal of Sister Freda's prophecy. There was another witness who had seen the same thing.

"I had a vision of Basil and a baby as well," sister Patsy interjected.

Patsy, the pastor's wife was the wife of Anne's father's school friend, and she knew all about the baby back home. They were sending a cryptic message to Basil through his wife, and he heard them loud and clear.

Basil did his best to convince Claudette that she had nothing to worry about, and eventually, she dropped the issue. For a while, Basil made monthly payments, but soon his practice fell on hard times. When the money dried up, Anne threatened to tell his wife about their daughter, Rita.

"Rita needs school fees," she demanded.

"I don't have it, Anne," he retorted.

"No problem, Basil. Let me call Claudette and see if she can chip in," she chided.

"You wouldn't dare!"

"Try me. Her work number is 718-200-5555."

"Or maybe I should send her a letter from the sweet island of Jamaica."

Basil and Claudette were not on the best of terms, and this was the last thing he needed.

"Okay, I'll get you the money," he hissed through clenched teeth.

It turned out that Anne was more devious than his wife. Rita was the last of Basil's children to come of age, and he had gone broke sending the others to university. But he had other plans for Rita. For her twentieth birthday, he promised her mother he would file her papers to come to America.

"I'm sending for Rita," he stated matter-of-factly.

"Just Rita?"

"Yes, only Rita," he snapped.

Basil was tired of being broke and had an opportunity to come into some money. He had taken on a client named Mr. Carleton, who had a sizable inheritance but no heirs. Basil befriended him and had been formulating a plan for the past few years. Initially, Mr. Carleton was apprehensive about Basil, but he kept showing up, offering free advice, and reassuring the old man that if he ever needed a lawyer, Esq. Basil Thompson was his guy. It took about a year of buttering up for the old nut to crack, but once he did, Basil became the go-to guy for all of Mr. Carleton's legal affairs.

One day, Mr. Carleton requested that Basil help him write a living will. This was his chance – the moment he had been waiting for. The only issue was how he was going to get Mr. Carleton to write him into his will. Basil schemed and plotted for weeks to come up with the perfect pitch. Eventually, he convinced Mr. Carleton to set up a living trust, of which Basil would be the fiduciary. The lawyer would oversee monies earmarked to start a charity for children in Mr. Carleton's hometown back in Jamaica.

What a coincidence – Mr. Carleton's hometown was the same place his bonus family lived. Little did the old man know that the charity Basil had in mind was the Basil Thompson Foundation, for which he was the sole beneficiary. After hours of discussion, Mr. Carleton gave Basil permission to draw up the paperwork. Everything was in place, but for some reason, the old man delayed signing off.

This was the last piece that needed to fall into place for him to secure his future, but the old man was dragging his feet. Basil dared not show any signs of discontent. It took everything in him to remain calm. The $100,000 that the old man had waiting gave Basil night fever. He found himself sitting up in bed, making mental notes of what he was going to do with the money.

All was going well until Devon Clarke. Devon had entered Mr. Carleton's life and altered the course of Basil's financial scheme. Devon was a young man from the neighborhood who grew to love Mr. Carleton like a grandfather. Over the years, the two became close, and when he graduated from high school, Mr. Carleton asked Basil to make some changes to his will. The will included a special clause that allowed Devon and his fiancée Jackie to access the funds if they achieved specific requirements.

Devon was unaware that he was the sole beneficiary of Mr. Carleton's small fortune. He only learned about his inheritance a few weeks after Mr. Carleton's passing. The lawyer realized he needed to find a way to get Devon and Jackie to break their side of the agreement.

Introducing Rita Thompson, daughter of Anne the Island Gyal. Rita knew very little about her father, and they rarely spoke on the phone when she was younger. Basil presented the opportunity as a father-daughter reunion, and Anne bought the story, relaying it to Rita as well. Anne had always wanted to go to America, but Basil never followed through on his promise. Although she never made it, she was pleased that her daughter would have the chance to go.

Chapter Six

Rita, a big fan of BET, watched the channel so intently it was almost like she was studying for a degree in pop culture. She envisioned herself walking and dressing just like her favorite artists. The moment her mother Anne informed her of her trip to America, thoughts of living the high life consumed her.

Rita turned around for one last goodbye to her mother, as she tugged her red and black suitcase toward the Carib-Am plane, waiting for her on the tarmac. Amidst the crowd, Anne's face stood out like a bird of paradise in a sea of green brush. This was Rita's first time away from home, her mother Anne, and the local boys who always called out to her whenever she went shopping. They named her "hot gyal Rita," and she loved it.

Arriving late that night, she was met by Basil in dark glasses and a trench coat. Although her reception wasn't quite like the movies, she was hopeful for the future. Her father had picked her up from the airport and brought her to Mrs. Hattie's home, introducing her as a friend's daughter. He entrusted the elderly woman to look after her before returning on a Saturday night to disclose the true reason he brought her to America.

Rita's association with her father, Basil, revolved entirely around his scheme, referred to as "the plan". The topic became synonymous with his visits, they did not have much to share beyond that. Basil coached and cajoled his daughter into compliance using pop culture images and promises of fame. Rita was convinced that "the plan" would succeed, and her bank account would be twenty thousand dollars richer.

She was now fully committed to "the plan" and did not care that her father was a scheming lawyer because she was his accomplice. Declining twenty thousand USD was out of the question, as it was more than her friends had back in Jamaica, and she was determined to obtain it.

-~-

Night crept in, and Rita remained seated on the front step with swollen feet and a bruised ego.

"Yuh wan sumtin fe eat Rita baby?"

"No thanks, Mrs. Hattie," Rita replied as she shifted painfully to her feet.

"I'm not that hungry tonight."

Despite her words, Rita was famished. The delicious scent of red peas soup wafted through the open window. Thyme and coconut milk mingled with the scent of kidney beans reminded Rita of home. She longed to be back in her bed, in her town with the boys that always told her how beautiful she was and, "how much dem woulda love fe wife her."

"Not hungry no sah, dat nuh good baby, come let Mrs. Hattie feed you," Mrs. Hattie urged, her well-placed bun remaining perfectly still as she shook her head. Rita never refused an offer to eat with Mrs. Hattie, she yearned for her comforting presence, but she couldn't chance it tonight. Agreeing to dinner meant facing questions, and questions meant the possibility that Basil Thompson's plan could be revealed. Without another word, Mrs. Hattie disappeared inside.

Rita hobbled towards the front door, her once flashy outfit now suffocating her. All she could think about was getting upstairs, taking a shower, and crawling into bed.

-~-

Basil stormed into his office throwing his keys amongst the folders on his cluttered desk. He was steaming mad and knew better than to go home. Claudette was a prosecuting attorney on and off the job and any sign of weakness in Basil's defense was sure to cause him stress. He was furious with Jackie, Devon and especially Rita.

He threw his long legs across the arm of his old couch and let out a wounded hungry lion roar. Arrr, *dat gyal Jackie is more desperate than I thought.* Basil grimaced because the thought of her caused him pain.

Rita, Rita, Rita; Basil called her name three times as if it would summon her to his presence. He banged his fist against the coffee table. *I did everything to get you ready for the job, but you cost me dearly just like your mother!* Basil looked around his office in disgust, he was too cheap to hire a cleaning service and charged Rita with keeping it tidy around there. "Not even that she could do," he barked.

"Everything dat gyal needed fe look good and seduce Devon me get har."

Nails done every two weeks. Hair every week. New outfits, shoes, and the latest perfume and still she messed up the plan. No one would have guessed that Basil, who by all appearances was a model citizen in the community, husband, father and professional would devise such a heartless scheme. Was he really in need of money or was there more to the story?

Basil rubbed his stomach realizing he had run off from the wedding before grabbing a plate. Hunger was setting in, and nothing made him more miserable than being hungry. He thumbed through a stack of local delivery flyers that he saves for occasions such as this. Chow Kitchen had a buy-one-get-one free coupon for chicken fried rice. The curry chicken with rice and peas sounded much better right now but that was out of the question. Chow's kitchen was quick and cheap, so he went with them. The clanking of his office phone ringing against the receiver frightened him. *Who could be calling at this time,* he pondered as he reached for the phone.

"Basil, Basil why are you still at the office on a Sunday night?" The voice was unmistakable, it was his wife Claudette calling to see where he had been all day.

"Look, Claudette," he replied, tired, and defeated. "I am working on a case and will be home soon. Is everything ok?"

"Well, yes I was just," she paused.

"I can't right now, I will be home later."

With that he hung up the phone without waiting for her reply.

Basil placed the call for his food, walked over to the safe situated in the corner of his office. It had been a while since he looked over Mr. Carleton's paper. Maybe there was something he missed or had forgotten to add to *the plan.* Inside the safe were two manilla envelopes, one with Mr. Carleton's will and the other with the reverse mortgage he had taken out on his family home. Claudette had no clue that her husband had a secret gambling addiction. She also did not know he took out a reverse mortgage on the house they paid off six years ago.

Basil was in deep; he owed a loan shark big money and needed the funds to pay off Tommy the Thumb. He secretly pulled out fifty thousand dollars from his family home to cover his debts but now Basil had a new problem. How was he going to make payments on the house with business in such a slump. That's when he met Mr. Carleton who trusted him to write up his paperwork.

Once Basil won Mr. Carleton's trust, he started siphoning his money. As if that wasn't enough, he forged quit claim deed paperwork for Mr. Carleton's house. According to the plan Basil would take charge of the inheritance, opening the charity and carrying out Mr. Carleton's last wish. By that time, he reasoned the old man would be long gone and none the wiser.

So, when Mr. Carleton asked Basil to add Devon and Jackie to his will; he had to act fast. Funnily enough Mr. Carleton insisted on having an additional party witness the changes to his will and here is another problem. If Basil doesn't come up with the money and make good on his agreement, he could lose his law practice and face jail time for fraud and financial exploitation of the elderly.

-~-

Basil took a bite of his chicken fried rice and grimaced.

"This is too greasy and doesn't even taste good." He washed it down with some iced tea.

"At least it got rid of the gas," he belched.

Basil winced as he thought back to the day's events, and the looming task of telling Tommy the Thumb about this month's payment only added to his mental anguish. He had scolded Rita earlier, hoping she would come up with a new plan for their next meeting. Basil had been working all night, every night and coming home late. He kept promising Claudette he would return early, but he never kept his word. Eventually, she stopped believing him.

Early that morning Basil stood outside his house rummaging through his pockets for his house keys. He considered the possibility of misplacing them in his car. Without warning, a stranger crept up behind him and pressed a cold, metallic object against his back.

"Basil ol' bwoy," he said, pausing between words for emphasis.

"You are running out of time."

With that, the man vanished into the night, leaving Basil standing frozen on his family's doorstep.

The next morning, he rose early and made his way straight to Rita's house.

"Rita!" he bellowed from beneath her window.

"Come out here now!"

Rita jolted out of bed at the sound of his voice, groggy from a sleepless night. She thought she might be dreaming at first, but when she peered through the corner of her red flannel curtains, she saw her father pacing frantically in the front yard. She scrambled to throw on a pair of sweats and her house slippers. The moment she opened the door, he pushed past her, demanding they go upstairs.

"Rita, what's your plan?" Basil flung his hands out to the side, demanding an answer.

"Is everything alright?" she asked, leaning against the door.

"I told you yesterday that you needed to make this work. The reality is we are running out of time, and if you don't come up with a plan soon, you and I will be going to jail."

"Jail?" Rita shrieked.

"What are you talking about?"

Things were getting serious fast. Rita knew about Basil's threat to deport her, but jail was a whole different level.

"Don't worry about that," he snapped.

"Just know that you and I will be having matching cells if you don't get Devon to break up with Jackie."

"I've been working on something," she said tentatively.

"If all goes well, they'll be broken up for good."

"Better," Basil huffed on his way out of the room.

Chapter Seven

Later that day, Rita checked in with Pam to see how Trevor was progressing with the plan. Trevor had instructed Pam to keep Rita in the dark and simply say, "It's all under control."

Unfortunately, with the information he had collected on Basil Thompson, it was going to be difficult to prevent Rita from getting involved in the drama. She wasn't entirely innocent herself. Despite awaiting Devon's agreement to his terms, Trevor continued to gather intel for the case.

Devon wrestled with the proposal. He wanted to give his marriage with Jackie a good start, but it appeared that he would have to keep one more secret for her own good. Newlyweds often struggled with financial issues that ultimately affected their marriage, and he didn't want that for them.

Trevor's demand of a fifteen percent was steep, Devon realized it was the only option. Devon called his cousin one night after work to inform him that he would stop by. The two met at went over the plan and agreed on the payout. The first order of business was to obtain a copy of Mr. Carleton's will.

"Mr. Thompson, it's Devon calling to follow up with you."

"Sorry we didn't get to talk at the wedding, but thanks for coming."

Devon left a message on Mr. Thompson's voicemail at the office. After a few hours, Basil called back. They awkwardly navigated through formalities, but when Basil asked if there was anything else he could do to help, Devon replied, "Yes, as a matter of fact, I wanted to stop by to get a copy of the will."

"Copy?"

"Of the will," he stuttered.

"Yes, I'll stop by later today."

He ended the call before Basil could object.

"What could have gotten into Devon?"

"Rita, Rita!" Basil bellowed.

"What's going on? Why is Devon requesting a copy of the will? Did you do something?"

"I have no idea," she shrugged.

Rita decided to play dumb for the time being until she could figure out why Devon had asked for the will. She and Basil went over possible reasons for the sudden change. Later that day, around three o'clock, the buzzer rang outside. Rita let the visitor in. It was Devon. Unlike his previous visits, she was not excited to see him. She had devised a plan to apologize for her actions and try to gain ground. He was alone surprisingly, and despite her shame and embarrassment, she couldn't deny that he still looked good.

"Mr. Clarke, glad to see you again," she bowed her head sheepishly.

"Hello Rita," Devon replied, stepping into the office with his head held high and face was still glowing from the joy of being a newlywed.

"Is Mr. Thomson in?"

"Yes, he is. I will call him in a minute," she hesitated but continued to plead.

"Please Devon, if you could give me a minute of your time."

Devon leaned back on one leg, shifting his body away from her desk.

"Please just hear me out."

"I wanted to apologize to you and your wife concerning my actions at your wedding. It was inappropriate of me to do what I did, and I am truly sorry. I wanted to meet with both of you to tell you this. I hope you accept my apology."

Apology, sorry? This was the last thing Devon had expected from Rita. He couldn't help but wonder if it was sincere given what Trevor had told him about Basil's plan.

"Rita," Basil hollered from his office.

"Who was at the door?"

Rita looked apologetically at Devon, motioning for him to forgive her and to keep the discussion between the two of them.

"It's Mr. Clarke," she shouted back.

Devon gave a quick nod, then directed his attention to Basil, who flung open his office door in a rush.

"Mr. Clarke, you're early," Basil exclaimed.

He handed Devon a manila envelope marked "Mr. Carleton's Will" with a few pages omitted and some information redacted. Basil didn't have enough time to take out all the details, but he also didn't want to draw suspicion.

"Is that all you needed for the day?"

"Yes, thanks."

Devon tugged the envelope from Basil's hand as it seemed he was reluctant to let it go.

"Now that Jackie and I are married, I look forward to our monthly disbursement," he affirmed.

"Yes, sure every month," Basil reiterated.

"As a matter of fact, I put the first check into the envelope for you."

Basil was trying to buy time and didn't want to give him too many reasons to come to his office before he figured things out. With that, Devon thanked them both and took his leave. Basil breathed a sigh of relief, giving Rita a look of distress before slinking back into his office and closing the door.

CHAPTER EIGHT

The crooked lawyer was consumed with thoughts of his misdeeds catching up to him. Each night he tossed and turned, struggling to sleep for more than a few hours. During the day, he found it difficult to focus on any of his other clients' needs.

What would that bwoy Devon want with a copy of the will? He considered every scenario, including the possibility of Rita double-crossing him. He dismissed the latter possibility, resolving that she could never be that crazy.

Whenever the sounds of doubt and trepidation became too much, Basil developed a habit of pacing. He paced at home, in the office, and at the park. One day, Trevor's investigators watched as he paced in the park for hours and reported the news back to him. This news confirmed everything Trevor needed to know. They had Basil just where they wanted him.

The sneaky man redacted some information from the contract, but he neglected to black out the second witness's name. Devon used the information to contact the lawyer who signed off on the will.

"He can't do this, it's illegal, and he can go to jail!"

"Jail?" Devon wrung his hands together; things were getting worse by the minute.

"If you want, we can file a formal complaint, and if push comes to shove, we can take it to trial."

What-ifs engulfed Devon's mind; he was drowning in this twisted tango between Rita, Basil, Trevor, and Jackie. Although he promised not to hold any more secrets, he had not told her about the latest developments.

"What do you suggest?"

"I suggest trying to see if you can get a confession from Basil or Rita," he leaned back confidently in his chair, biting the tip of his glasses.

"A confession?"

"What do we need them to say, and how would this affect whether this case goes to trial?"

"Basil needs to admit he is in violation of the contract and has compromised his duties as a sworn public official."

"As a matter of fact, he can be disbarred, lose his practice, go to jail, and or be put on probation."

Devon thanked the lawyer, assured him he would be in touch, and took his leave.

His gut churned and he wished Mr. Carleton was here so he could give him some advice, but to no avail, he was on his own. He toyed with the idea of telling Jackie and conveniently leaving out the part about having to pay Trevor a *thank-you* gift. Why complicate things if he didn't have to?

At home, Jackie was waiting with dinner prepared. The newlyweds had barely made it off the aisle when all this drama took place. Things were tight financially, and neither Devon nor Jackie had been able to land a job, so they watched every dime until something panned out. Dinner was a humble bowl of lentil soup, and Devon didn't complain; he ate most of his meal in silence.

"Devon, babes, what's wrong?" his wife gently rested her hand on his.

"You've been quiet since you got in."

"Everything is," he hesitated, contemplating how much of the situation he wanted to share.

Devon shared with Jackie everything Trevor and the lawyer told him about Basil Thompson's funny business. Jackie, in true fashion, was ready to fight. She never forgave Rita for the stunt she pulled and was ready to have her and the lawyer pay.

"I guess we'll see them in court!"

That was exactly what Devon was afraid of.

-~-

One Wednesday morning, Basil's office received an official notice to appear. Rita quickly signed off for the envelope and handed it to her father without a word. Basil immediately burst out of his office, flinging the paper that Rita held just moments earlier on her desk.

"What! That bwoy have some nerve!"

She calmly slid the paper off the desk and read it. Her father was being sued for theft, mismanagement of funds, exploitation, and financial abuse of the elderly.

The scandal rocked the entire community, leaving Basil Thompson, the thieving lawyer, with nowhere to hide. With leaks springing up everywhere, he found himself on the brink of going mad. Tommy the Thumb was the first to catch him slipping, his crew running up on Basil to give him a visit he wouldn't forget. He spent a few weeks in the hospital and was relieved to get away even if it was under the watchful eye of medical staff.

The looming lawsuit filed by Devon was a big problem, and he had no real defense. In true Basil fashion, he appeared in court and opted to defend himself. He pleaded for the mercy of the court and painted Rita as the temptress who concocted the entire plot. He accused her of illegally accessing and forging the paperwork. Basil testified against Rita, suggesting that she was an illegal immigrant and should be deported back to the island and never allowed to return.

Basil Thompson put on quite a show, leaving everyone in the room impressed. Rita was shocked by her own father's betrayal, as he testified against her. Fortunately, her mother had warned her about Basil's treachery, and although Rita was hesitant to believe her, she took precautions. Rita had copies of her father's underhanded dealings, which she used to prove his guilt beyond a reasonable doubt.

Despite his attempts to sway the jury, they found him guilty and sentenced him to four years in minimum security, five years of probation, and a payment of fifty thousand dollars in restitution. By the time he was released, he had lost everything – his job, his home, and his family. Claudette divorced him and kept the house after discovering all his misdeeds. He was forced to move into his elderly mother's basement.

After the trial, Rita was left alone. Without Basil's financial support, she could not maintain her lifestyle in America. She considered returning home, but she did not want to do so with her tail between her legs. During the trial, she learned that Basil had not filed her paperwork; instead, he kept extending her visitor visa, suggesting that he had every intention of sending her back when the job was complete.

Rita met a friend who said she should try and find an American to marry. Although she had heard of people coming to America and marrying to get papers, she never thought it would be her. If she were to consider something like this, who would it be and when? With only two months left on her visa, she had to make a move quickly.

While Basil was still in jail, he would often place collect calls to Rita, demanding that she do this or that. One day, he asked her to stop by the office to meet a lawyer friend of his who was working on his case. Despite all that her father had done to her, she agreed. The office had been locked up since Basil went away, and it was stuffier and smellier than ever. Rita tried airing it out before their guest arrived.

"This is the best I can get it," she concluded, taking out the overflowing trash to the back.

The buzzer rang, and she hurriedly made her way back up front to open the door. In walked a handsome, slender twenty-something professional in a pinstripe suit with gold cufflinks. He was fresh out of law school, looking for an opportunity to make a name for himself. Rita perked up at the sight of him.

"Mr.?" she paused, waiting for him to share his name.

"Esq. Blackman," he smirked, shaking her hand.

"Your father sent me for some files."

"Oh, yes, files." Rita ran to her father's desk and rummaged through the files on his desk.

"Thanks," he replied as she handed him the stack.

"Leaving so soon?" she inquired.

"Why? Is there more?" the handsome man looked around the office.

"No, that's it, I think. But I was wondering if we could talk."

Rita wanted to know more about the attractive stranger, so she offered him a drink, which he declined.

"So," he asked, casing the office, "what does your father plan to do with this place?"

"I'm not sure."

"This would be perfect for me to start my practice." The wheels in his head began to turn, and he figured that in exchange for his help on the case, Basil could give him permission to operate out of his unused office and have access to Rita, his secretary. When Esq. Blackman next visited Basil, he proposed the idea, knowing that he had the upper hand. Basil reluctantly agreed in hopes that his new lawyer would get him out earlier.

Esq. Blackman started coming around more, and he and Rita cleaned up the office, giving it an entire makeover. She toned down her dress and presented herself as someone ready to settle down, hoping to catch a man. Their connection was magnetic, and before long, Esq. Blackman was dipping into Rita's files. Rita soon became pregnant by him, and it was at this time that she told him about her immigration dilemma and what her father, Basil Thompson, had done.

Blackman stopped working on Basil's case and promised Rita that he would marry her and help straighten out her immigration issues. One year later, she was the proud mother of a baby girl and the proud holder of her green card.

-~-

A decade had passed since the will drama, and Devon and Jackie were now planning to relocate to a bigger house in sunny Florida. On their wedding anniversary, they received a lump sum of $50,000 in their account, the remaining half being paid by Basil Thompson in incriments. Devon, without consulting Jackie, transferred five percent to his cousin, banking on the rental income to make up for it. With a new job offer in Florida, the couple were thrilled to have a fresh start in a warmer climate. Their excitement grew as they learned that Jackie was pregnant again and a bigger home was necessary for their growing family.

Chapter Nine

"Babes, I'm starving," Devon said, looking into the empty refrigerator. The couple had packed all their pots and pans, so ordering out was their only option. Jackie wasn't a fan of street food, but she was willing to make an exception.

"How about pizza?" she said waving a local pizzeria flyer.

"Chinese sounds better," Devon countered.

"Let's flip a coin."

"Heads for pizza, tails for Chinese."

The coin landed on tails, and they ordered veggie fried rice and chicken wings. Thirty minutes later, the doorbell rang, and he searched his pockets for a tip to give the delivery man. When he opened the door, he and the driver were stunned. Devon reached forward to collect his food, but the driver stood motionless, except for his piercing eyes that watched him intently. Devon intended to shut the door without saying a word, but the driver put out his hand for the tip that was now balled up in Devon's palm.

"No tip?" the driver asked.

This man has no limits, he thought, shaking his head.

Basil, the ex-lawyer-turned-deliveryman, spun around, flung his delivery bag under his arm, jumped in his old jalopy, and drove away.

Jackie and the children stepped out of the kitchen, carrying plates and forks, hungry for their meal. Though the aroma of the food filled their noses, they couldn't spot it anywhere. Jackie searched for the classic Chinese takeout box with red letters, but it was nowhere to be found. In fact, Devon was nowhere to be seen either. Just then, he came in from outside.

"Devon, where's the food?" Jackie asked, confused since she was almost certain she heard the bell ring.

"You know what, Jackie? I decided to order pizza instead.

The Chinese food looked a bit spoiled," Devon replied.
In truth, it was Basil's face that had dampened Devon's appetite. Jackie rubbed her pregnant belly, searching for a spot on the floor to sit, while Devon looked over at his lovely wife and decided against telling her that Basil was back. He couldn't find a good enough reason to upset his expectant wife.

Moments later, the doorbell rang, and the pizza man arrived with breadsticks and a New York pizza pie half-pineapple, half-olive. The family sat at the kitchen table, ready to enjoy their final meal in Mr. Carleton's house.

Devon and Jackie were busy loading their belongings into the moving truck the next morning. While he was focused on the task at hand, Jackie was wandering around the house, lost in thought about everything and anything. A few days earlier, Devon had asked Trevor to help with the heavy furniture, but he declined, citing other commitments. It turns out that he was still upset about only receiving a portion of the *thank you* money because Basil stole it. Last night, after dinner, Jackie's parents picked up the children to spend some quality time before the family's departure. Mama was sad to learn that the family was moving away from them, but she understood they needed more space.

Jackie rarely had a moment to herself, so she was grateful for the chance to sit down and take a breather. As she rested at the corner table in the kitchen, which was the only piece of furniture left, she reflected on her life. Suddenly, the phone rang from an unknown number, and she debated whether to answer.

Ultimately, she picked up, and a distressed voice called out her name from the other end.

"Jackie Brown, I see you."

It had been a decade since anyone had called her by that name, and the caller's identity remained a mystery. Devon and the neighbor entered the house to collect the table. Before leaving, Devon reminded her to grab the last box, which was carefully labeled as "fragile" and filled with crystal hangings and folded lilac curtains.

"Yes, my love, I won't forget."

Jackie replied, her mind still preoccupied with the mysterious phone call.

EMUNAH Y'SRAEL

Island Twist

A Carib-American Tale of Love & Culture

Copyright © 2023 by Emunah Y'srael

Acknowledgments

Thanks to the Creator for life and the ability to reach people with my writing. Thanks to my parents who have worked and supported and encouraged my siblings and I to shoot for the stars. Thanks to my husband and children who continue to be supportive and patient during the process of my many ventures. To my extended family and friends much gratitude for all that you have contributed to this process. I extend my sincere gratitude to everyone who has read and will read this work. My hope is that it brings joy, healing, and light to your world.

About the Author

Emunah (Faith) is a successful entrepreneur, author, and devoted mother of four wonderful children. Her life has been a journey of self-discovery and personal growth, as she confronts the emotional challenges and tribulations that life presents. Emunah's unwavering faith in the Creator, as well as the strength of peace, laughter, and honesty, are all values she holds dear. As she travels the globe, Emunah immerses herself in adventure and education, constantly learning and evolving.

Emunah Y'srael

Let's Link Up!

www.open-book-media.com

@openbookmedia.444

Printed in Great Britain
by Amazon